CENTERING PRAYERS

CENTERING PRAYERS

A One-Year Daily Companion for Going Deeper into the Love of God

PETER TRABEN HAAS

PARACLETE PRESS
BREWSTER, MASSACHUSETTS

2021 Fifth Printing
2019 Fourth Printing
2017 Third Printing
2014 Second Printing
2013 First Printing

Centering Prayers: A One-Year Daily Companion for Going Deeper into the Love of God

ISBN 978-1-61261-415-1

Library of Congress Cataloging-in-Publication Data

Haas, Peter Traben.
Centering prayers : a one-year daily companion for going deeper into the love of God / Peter Traben Haas.
pages cm
Includes bibliographical references.
ISBN 978-1-61261-415-1 (trade pb)
1. Prayers. I. Title.
BV245.H215 2013
242'.8—dc23 2013024326

10 9 8 7 6 5

Published by Paraclete Press
Brewster, Massachusetts
www.paracletepress.com
Printed in the United States of America

To the mentors who have,
in different ways,
formed my life for the good:

RICHARD HAAS

BOB ALLAN

STUART BRISCOE

JIM RUMSEY

DAVID KEARNS-PRESTON

JOE STOWELL

WALTER BELFIELD

GENE DOLBY

JOE COYNER

DAVID JONES

TIM COOK

VAN HOISINGTON

BELOVED, SOURCE OF LIFE:

We come from you and return to you,
and in between we learn how to love.

You are with us, and
beyond the gray veil of perception,
we are with you.

CONTENTS

PREFACE

Be a student of that vibrant edge where our inner life meets the world . . . where we all live on [the] shore between the depths of being and the dangers of experience.

—Mark Nepo, *The Exquisite Risk*

I feel particularly grateful to be writing this preface from the St. Albertino guest room at the New Camaldoli Hermitage in Big Sur, California. I write with a majestic view of the Pacific Ocean—today, an opaque blue capped with white runners as far as I can see from this high hillside vantage. Silence surrounds me, except for the faint and constant roar of the ocean that sounds to me like a distant highway. Of course, it's not the sound of cars and traffic to which I am so accustomed, living in the city. Rather, it is the sound of the sea singing its praises as it meets the end of its world and the beginning of ours.

I have come to this Benedictine hermitage as an interlude. I recently left a beloved pastoral role in Austin,

Texas, to begin a new pastorate in Waterloo, Iowa. Like the liminal meeting place of sea and land, I too am in between the boundaries of ending and beginning. And so, I have retreated to the silence in a place of vast beauty.

Here in the silence grace has ministered to me. Both tears and laughter have bubbled up in my prayer times as I release the life I am leaving behind. I peer across the sea and find myself pondering all that was and also what might be.

From the solitude of this retreat I remember the quiet Austin mornings when these centering prayers were written. I cherish those years of interior growth and especially the community of spiritual friends who supported my flourishing.

My own prayer is that the words in this book nurture you beyond the written word into the womb of silence experienced through some method of receptive prayer, such as centering prayer or the Jesus prayer. They are shared here with the wish that they might nourish a deepening experience of God's love, especially when read as a prelude or postlude to periods of contemplative prayer.

The prayers are sent forth in printed form with the hope that they reach brothers and sisters of Spirit gazing across their own oceans of devotion. We are connected through word and silence, growing ever deeper in God's love.

ABOUT THE PRAYERS

The brevity of most of the prayers is an intentional effort in service of a contemplative prayer practice.

Although almost all of the prayers use the first-person singular "I" instead of the more universal first-person plural "we," I recognize that our prayers are always in some way interconnected with the human family, across all times and places. Our communion of prayer is not limited by generations or locations. Prayer integrates time and eternity, earth and heaven, and transcends any one person's silent devotion and evocations of pain, ecstasy, or earnest plea.

Thus, while this simple book of prayers will most likely be used by individuals devotionally, at no point are we ever really alone in this sighing of spirit to Spirit. We are praying as well as being prayed, as a continuing living universal body becoming love.

JANUARY

It is as if God says to me:

Your radiance cannot be hidden by your mistakes or by any external situation you may be experiencing.

Your life is hidden with me.

Rejoice a little today in this knowledge.

My love changes everything.

JANUARY 1

Standing on your everlasting foundation

O God Who Calls Me into Life:

Standing on the strength of your everlasting foundation, I cast forth my seeds of intention into the days unfolding before me this New Year.

Strengthened by the web of shared yet unseen hopes connected in silence, I see each choice as victory and the days to come as vibrant.

In Christ, it is and shall be.

Amen.

JANUARY 2

You are the One

Lord Jesus, Living Christ:

Empty, I am filled.

Heavy, I am carried.

Lost, I am guided.

Imprisoned, I am released.

Angry, I am calmed.

Anxious, I am given peace.

Alone, I am visited.

Hopeless, I am reminded of miracles.

Hungry, I am fed.

Thirsty, I am quenched.

On and on the reversals go—you are the One who turns my water into wine. You touch my life with your Word and say, *Be free. Be filled. Be light. Be found. Be peace. Be abundance. Be love. Be joy. Be life.*

Amen.

JANUARY 3

Resting with you

Spirit of God:

I begin this year with the simplicity of silence.

Resting with you, I become myself again.

Amen.

JANUARY 4

Replace my fears with love

Loving God:

Replace my fears with love.

Where I fear lack, bring abundance.

Where I fear sickness, bring wholeness.

Where I fear others, bring reconciliation.

Where I fear being wrong, bring freedom.

Forgive the ways I use fear as an excuse to limit love.

Forgive me when I use my thoughts and words as tools of fear.

You are love.

Humanity is your beloved.

I often forget this in my fears. Today, I wish to remember.

Amen.

■ ■ ■

JANUARY 5

My first awakened song

God of New Life:

You invite me into your presence of love to know myself in the embrace of others. Such communion is my first awakened song, lifted high to Christ's throne, table, and touch. And I am healed.

Amen.

■ ■ ■

JANUARY 6

I remember your love

Loving God:

I wish to be in love with humanity by embracing the human experience with my brothers and sisters.

Like the ancient Magi, help me recognize and receive the divine presence in another. Give to me a melting sweetness that dissolves separations, bringing a sense of unity with everything.

I remember your love that wishes to appear through me today as Epiphany.

Amen.

JANUARY 7

You welcome me into your love

Loving God:

In all my movement, you are present.

When I am busy and burdened, you welcome me into your rest.

When I am cold and alone, you invite me into the warmth of your love.

While many ideas are available to humanity, when I am at rest and in love with you, I discover that your living presence is beyond idea; it is experience.

I welcome this connecting gift.

I receive your warmth, life, love, and peace.

Amen.

JANUARY 8

In your silent grace

Beloved of the Heart:

Underneath every burden I feel is a blessing that I do not.

Loosen with gentleness each emotional knot tied too tight in the tug-of-war called life.

In your silent grace, I receive the gentleness to hold my brokenness with acceptance and my dreams with trust.

You are with me despite the tensions made tight by the living of life.

Underneath each burden is your invitation to see with different sight.

Beyond the perception of the situation and the emotion of the moment is the deepest reality of all: I am with you and you are with me.

Help me affirm today that in Christ nothing can separate me from you—including my own thoughts and feelings.

Amen.

■ ■ ■

JANUARY 9

To feel the heat of your heart

Home of My Heart:

God of all who worry and wander, draw me home to your hearth.

When the universe appears cold, my heart tells me there is a living warmth called love.

In prayer, I wish to feel your heart blazing with a heat that holds everything together while fears seek to crack me apart.

In and through Jesus Christ, fire of my heart, fusion of loving fellowship, help of humankind.

Amen.

JANUARY 10

Bring wholeness

Source of My Strength:

Bring wholeness to the fragmentation of my thoughts, feelings, and actions.

Release my constrictions against others, myself, and your divine love.

Set me free with the power of your love, healed through surrender into your ever-sustaining grace.

Amen.

JANUARY 11

You are the first light in the depths of the deep

God of Mercy:

You who are the first light in the depths of the deep, kindly shine unexpected blessings upon my life outstretched to you.

Draw me into the silence so as to feel your closeness, and send me into the world attuned to the movement of your mercy, beyond the cultural swings of all or nothing, winning or losing, peace or conflict.

Amen.

JANUARY 12

Sealed with your strong, unflinching love

Beloved:

I take you for better or worse, richer or poorer, in sickness or in health, into eternity.

Sealed with your strong, unflinching love, I am free to be present to the world and my responsibilities, assured that you are with me and I am with you.

Amen.

JANUARY 13

Soften my edges

O Lord, Giver of This Journey:

Soften my edges as your grace forms me.

Uncoil me by your incomprehensible love and grace.

How else shall I reply to such blessings than to kneel with adoration as you gift me with the inheritance of your healing Word?

Amen.

JANUARY 14

The unshakable silence of love

Abba:

Some days I remember I need more help than I realize.

Today, I surrender to your grace.

You are holding all who suffer with the unshakable silence of love.

Each moment is a gift received, each human a part of your whole.

In the name of Jesus Christ, who holds us all together in grace.

Amen.

JANUARY 15

My inner life grounded in you

Almighty God:

As life on this planet becomes tumultuous, I wish to have my inner life grounded in you through Christ by the Spirit.

I begin this moment, consenting to your presence and action within.

Amen.

JANUARY 16

With a certain strength of love

Lord Jesus, Living Christ:

Strengthen me in love.

Nourish me in faith.

Draw me into your life.

I request your shield of favor so as to proceed today with a certain strength of love.

Amen.

JANUARY 17

The power of mercy lifting minds

O God Who Surrounds the World with Justice and Mercy:

Thank you for the gift of words that do their transforming work through the voices of prophets and martyrs of truth.

Thank you for the fierce mercy of nonviolent resistance in the face of shame, torture, and ignorance.

Thank you for the power of mercy lifting my mind beyond limited boundaries into the realm of deeper love and understanding.

I humbly offer my life as a continuation of this voice and work of truth—to birth mercy in the face of injustice.

Through Christ, the merciful one, I pray.

Amen.

JANUARY 18

Let the kingdom of my heart open

Beloved Wisdom, Holy Compassion:

I wish to feel the touch of your blessing today in the empty places of my being.

Where there is lack of wisdom, love, or goodness, bring insight, compassion, and open-heartedness.

Let the kingdom of my heart open and expand toward someone new today, releasing that which represses me in self-absorption and freeing me to live in your presence.

Amen.

JANUARY 19

The miracle of your life in me

Spirit of God:

Move in my life. Unfold your growth in me turn by turn in an open spiral of development.

I am warmed by the miracle of your life in me.

Amen.

JANUARY 20

A vessel of adoration

Loving God:

Use every person and complexity to anoint me as a vessel of adoration, throwing off the light of love instead of perpetuating the frictions of personality.

Amen.

JANUARY 21

The inwardness of my being

Lord of Life:

I wish to feel invigorated today by your love that leads me into wholeness. Connect the current of your life with the inwardness of my being.

I wish to be well by connecting with you in my heart-center, receiving abundance so as to share it abundantly.

In and through Christ this can and shall be.

Amen.

JANUARY 22

Inside the silence

Lord God of All Creation:

In your grace, my wrong turns become unexpected paths.

Inside this grace, you enable my surrender, and there I find your love.

Inside your love, I find silence.

Inside the silence, you are and I am.

Amen.

JANUARY 23

Anoint me with the warmth of divine love

Living Love:

Anoint me with the warmth of divine love, made visible in the exchange of my words and glances toward you and others.

Turn my mere curiosities of faith into true God-devotion.

Amen.

JANUARY 24

Lifting my sorrows into joy

Holy Spirit:

Transform my private Scripture reading into your personal love with me in the inner chamber of my heart, lifting my sorrows into joy. Turn on the lights of radiant wisdom in me through your life-giving Word.

Amen.

JANUARY 25

At the center of my being

Abba:

I begin this day with gratitude for the gift that is hidden in my center.

Remind me in the silence of surrender that I am connected by more than what keeps me apart.

Help me see that at the center of all that lives is a small piece of the very beginning, which was with you and is now your Word always with us.

Amen.

JANUARY 26

In the shelter of your presence

Beloved:

Let me dwell in the shelter of your presence.

There is no end to my falling into your love, yet your love holds firm.

Life and all its situations will not shelter me.

Nor will my successes.

Therefore, today I make the inward turn to silence to feel your strength as the energy for all my doings and for my deepest rest.

In Christ, soul of my soul, I pray.

Amen.

JANUARY 27

Lead me home

Most Merciful and Loving Abba:

Thank you for always hearing my heart as it rises up in prayer. Nurture in me today the awareness of your closeness.

I wish to grow in consciously chosen mercy and love, beyond my likes, dislikes, and opinions. Help me hold others' truth in reverence.

When I fall back into forgetfulness and wander into judgment, lead me home to your loving embrace, which extends perfectly to all.

Amen.

■ ■ ■

JANUARY 28

Transform me into love

Lord God of Light and Love:

Warmed by the Son inside, I see your wonders and melt to the life of feeling.

Awaken in me the desire for you.

Free me from the fears that cripple.

Connect me to the joy that brings freedom.

Transform me into love.

Open me to wisdom and live through me as the way, the truth, and the life.

Amen.

JANUARY 29

Miracles of love and supply will arrive

O Path of Life, Journey of Love:

I live in the field of wholeness in which I can awaken and become aware that you wish to live through me. I welcome the experiences of this day as a recognition that whatever is occurring is perfect for my transformation in Christ.

Amen.

JANUARY 30

Only love heals

Most Merciful Sustainer of My Life:

Your love is the holy meaning of life.

Your love surges to bring all life into being and carries me into your promised beyond.

Your love heals broken hearts and mends fractured homes and nations.

Your love speaks in the middle of the night when I feel all alone.

Your love stays with me when no one else will.

Your love remembers when everyone else forgets.

Your love gives third chances, again and again.

Your love sees a life of beauty when others only see emotional baggage.

For every marriage wandering.

For every child hurting.

For every friend alone.

For every spouse grieving.

For every wound healing.

For every heart longing.

For every soul passing on.

For every parent worrying.

For every teen questioning.

For every need seeking.

There is and shall be love.

In this Trinity of affirmation, love shall be.

God is love.

We come from God.

We return to God and in between we become love.

All things come and go. Love endures forever. [1]

Amen.

JANUARY 31

Inspire a connected courage

God of Unending Welcome:

Urge my heart into honesty.

Where I feel mocked, inspire a connected courage that feels the oneness of human life beyond all our differences.

Where I feel less than perfect, remind me that nothing can separate me from your love—including other people's judgments or my own doubts and fears.

This I pray through Christ, the one and the many.

Amen.

FEBRUARY

It is as if God says to me:

Whatever path of loneliness or loss you may be traveling, miracles of love and supply will arrive. Your heart is beating; your lungs are breathing; your mind is bright with conscious light.

Beyond your thoughts of lack and longings for love is a truth of my reality: my love has always met and will always meet all your needs. The sea will part. The storm will calm. My presence changes everything.

But you must change your inner world of how you see things. And that is the secret to your freedom. A dirty window makes the world look fouled. The mind's eyes are the window to your soul. Perception is the path. Truth is the light that guides the way. If you wish a different path, cleanse your perception with my truth.

To change the way you take in impressions is to change your life. No one else can do this for you. I give Truth. You are invited to put it to use. For this, my grace abounds.

FEBRUARY 1

Awaken me more into the realm of faith

Lord Jesus Christ:

Awaken me more into the realm of faith that I might feel your power working through me as a vessel of divine healing.

Let me be the conduit of your healing touch. Give me the courage in that moment to forget myself and simply remember you.

Amen.

■ ■ ■

FEBRUARY 2

The majesty of your love

Abba:

As I dwell in the majesty of your love, I hope to become a participant of your unfolding story.

Write your words deep in my heart. Seal understanding and inner meaning in the chambers of my mind.

I wish to recognize wisdom, receive it, and dedicate myself to it.

I wish to educate myself in the temple of your truth and know beyond believing.

Amen.

FEBRUARY 3

You turn my failures into perfect love

God of Mercy:

You turn my failures into perfect love.

Help me remember this truth and to forget all things to the contrary.

I am not defined by the surface of things. I am defined by the One from whom I came and to whom I return, and you, O God, are the essence of love.

Amen.

FEBRUARY 4

Your hidden love at the center of my being

O Most Sacred Life of Christ:

Unveil the secret of your hidden love at the center of my being. Awakened, I welcome your center holding me.

Amen.

FEBRUARY 5

Graceful centering in the silence

God of Perfect Provision:

Your seeds of truth feed me on the journey to the banquet of your presence. Bring me into the balance of being one with you through Christ by the Spirit, and through the graceful centering of your silence feed the hunger and thirst you have placed within me.

Today, I wish to experience your love in the garden of your presence—and also in the city of humankind.

Amen.

FEBRUARY 6

In your love I live

God of Resurrection Light:

In your love I live, and in your life I am lifted out of the darkness of every difficulty.

Today, I pray to deeply remember that you are drawing me out of the shadows and filling my heart with a song of prayer: *When in darkness with no light but that which in my heart does burn, you, Lord Jesus Christ, bring the warmth of love.*

Amen.

FEBRUARY 7

Your blaze is a mighty silence

Great Son of God in the Heavens:

Your blaze is mighty, its power overwhelming.

Your shining edge is all I see in the silence, and even that radiant sliver hurts the eyes of my heart. I'm turning to you in prayer now as if to shake the lightning shock away.

Amen.

FEBRUARY 8

Recognize, receive, and remember your love

Eternal and Loving God:

Superficial life attempts to smother the truth that I am a chosen beneficiary of your love.

Help me remember today. Help me wake up more fully to it.

May I recognize, receive, and remember your love, despite all external evidence to the contrary.

Your love operates under a different set of rules that I don't comprehend. But I can feel it, and that makes all the difference.

Amen.

■ ■ ■

FEBRUARY 9

You are the space in between every breath

God Beyond Words and Understanding:

You are the silence underneath my waiting for some sign that life has a purpose.

You are the space in between every breath and sob and shout of sorrow, grief, or desperation.

You are the hunger and the food that compels my search for meaning.

You are everything—even if I live as if you are nothing.

Draw me now into the inner heart of this life, knowing beyond knowing the Christ-way, truth, and life of your presence.

Amen.

FEBRUARY 10

Risen, unconquerable light amidst the shadows

God of My Life:

I am not just flesh and bones but living breath, rising up into relationship and Son-song, worship and service. My future is unveiled in the open tomb, embraced by emptiness assuring that everything in life is my teacher. Even death holds my hand, instructing me in the way of my Teacher, risen, unconquerable light amidst the shadows.

Amen.

FEBRUARY 11

Cultivate in me a skillfulness to love

Source of My Being:

Stretch me beyond the demand for personal advantages.

Increase my capacity for silence. Diminish my negative reactivity.

Teach me the balanced way of holding life-tensions with hope.

Expand my tolerance for ambiguity and acceptance of others just where they are, reducing my addiction to making others wrong.

Cultivate in me a skillfulness to love, using every situation and life experience as a means for growth toward your likeness.

Amen.

FEBRUARY 12

The truth I can become

Lord Jesus Christ:

You know the truth I can become.

You show me the way to purity of heart.

Open my eyes to see beyond the senses. I wish to perceive your presence and participate in the experience of knowing ultimate reality, blessed with the vision of you, living Trinity, Father, Son, and Holy Spirit.

Amen.

FEBRUARY 13

To feel your life at the center of my being

Lord God of All Creation:

I wish to feel your life at the center of my being.

Transform the living water of my life into the red wine of holy love.

Do this transformation in me, and give me the courage to share what I have been given.

Amen.

FEBRUARY 14

Your life-giving Word in the silence of surrender

God My Beloved:

I belong to you.

You take me as your beloved into the unknown of this and every moment.

Guard my heart. Increase my devotion. Protect me from the temptations that distract my attention from your presence, sapping the impulse and vitality to praise, listen, and adore your life-giving Word in the silence of surrender.

Amen.

FEBRUARY 15

Deepen my attention to silence

To the Living God I Pray:

Deepen my attention to silence at the center of this inward breath, drawing me beyond the surface of things into the heart of your Christ.

Let this occur in the midst of my commerce and movement, conversation and encounters.

I wish to truly awaken to my hidden vocation as a temple of your Spirit, becoming an embodied messenger of your love, grace, and goodness.

In your most holy threefold name, Father, Son, and Holy Spirit, I pray.

Amen.

FEBRUARY 16

Held through the sways of life by your grace

To the God Who Is Here I pray:

The fullness of your Word feeds me, transforming seeds of truth into miracles of love and joy.

In this moment, I feel and remember who I am. Help me live according to this deep-seated knowledge. I wish to feel held through the sways of life by your grace.

Amen.

FEBRUARY 17

Touched by the presence of your victory

Beloved:

Pour out your Spirit upon me today so that all my suffering might be touched by the presence of your victory.

Amen.

FEBRUARY 18

Your grace that connects

God My Center:

Throughout this day, bring your grace in the midst of aggravations to my spirit.

Help me remain in contact with your grace that connects all despite the attacks of words and gestures by others.

When I feel swamped by the frustrations and difficulties of life that seem personally against me, help me enter into your kingdom of love, available always right here and now.

Amen.

FEBRUARY 19

The peace of mind to remain silent

God of Peace:

Between the extremes of hatred and love, bring peace into my relationships.

Lessen the pendulum swings of negative emotions in my body, mind, and emotions.

Where I am unable to say anything that nurtures love, give me the peace of mind to remain silent.

Through Christ, the Prince of Peace, I pray.

Amen.

FEBRUARY 20

The warmth of divine love

Holy Spirit of God:

Anoint me with the warmth of your divine love made visible in the exchange of words and glances.

Turn my curiosities of faith into devotion, and help me see others with the mind of Christ.

Amen.

FEBRUARY 21

The open-hearted surrender to grace

God My Center:

Your ever-increasing love is offered even through the upheavals of life. You hold the center as life spins, taking its turns from one generation to the next.

I listen in the silence for the peace that can't be understood or shaken. It is your life-giving word meeting me face to face in the open-hearted surrender to grace that each moment offers.

I begin this day saying yes to the strength of your center.

Amen.

■ ■ ■

FEBRUARY 22

Your loving presence enduring

God of Abraham and Sarah:

I give thanks for this day and the gift of life. While I may not understand why things are the way they are, I can feel your loving presence enduring even amidst my uncertainty, and so I pray:

Amidst temptations, give me the will to choose what is right. In my hurry, give me patience to remain silent as I wait for wisdom.

When blessed, give me gratitude to recognize how much I have been given.

Amen.

FEBRUARY 23

Deeper into Abba's love

Lord Jesus, Living Christ:

You returned good for evil, blessings for curses, love for hate, and acceptance for accusations.

You have shown me that the way to transformation is through surrender—giving up my will to power, success, and control.

Draw me into inner solitude and silence so that I might follow you deeper into Abba's love.

Amen.

FEBRUARY 24

Hold me close

Loving God:

Seal me from negative thoughts and feelings.

By sacrament, Word, and Spirit, neutralize this negativity lest it spread.

I wish to have my feeling of "I" in you and not in myself, my situations, or my turbulent moods that ebb and flow with life events.

Hold me close.

Amen.

FEBRUARY 25

Toward the infinite vastness of Jesus Christ

O God, My Mother-Father:

I begin this day in the safety of your ever-present love.

Shift my attention away from just myself and toward the infinite vastness of the living Christ.

Amen.

■ ■ ■

FEBRUARY 26

I embrace my role as a reflection of your glory

Sophia Spirit:

My mind is a center for reception. Enlighten my every cell.

Give me the wisdom to see what needs to be said, done, and undone.

I embrace my role as a reflection of your glory. Imbue my countenance with the joyful inheritance I have been given as a co-heir with Christ.

Amen.

■ ■ ■

FEBRUARY 27

The deepest truth you are inviting me to remember

God of Transformation:

You call me into the heart to listen for your voice, ignoring the chatter of my mind. Help me to observe and not identify with the inner dialog, especially when it is negative and self-critical.

I wish to personally experience your Word feeding my ongoing transformation with truth and wisdom, revealing the deepest truth you are inviting me to receive.

Amen.

FEBRUARY 28

Where I end and you begin

Transforming Trinity:

Help me accept your invitation to live in you so deeply that I can't tell where I end and you begin.

Amen.

FEBRUARY 29, LEAP YEAR

The becoming of the world needs me

God Whose Name Is "I Am":

Help me see how the becoming of the world needs me. Tune my heart into the calling that I uniquely am here to receive and embody.

Give inspiration for the days when I feel lost and uncertain how to contribute from the center of my being, in union with the eternal "I Am" that you are.

Amen.

MARCH

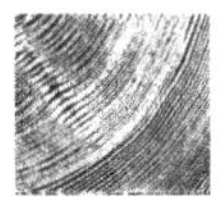

It is as if God says to me:

I am the eternal waiting for all to return home to me.

Your arrival is not to a place per se. It is to a relationship.

Your prayer supports your return and our growing relationship.

MARCH 1

I may not feel your grace right now

God Who Lifts Me Up:

Although I may not feel your grace right now.

Although I may be identified with negative feelings at this moment.

Although there may be little apparent reason for my senses to believe.

Nevertheless my failures and falls are my truest teachers of transformation.

You, O my God, are using all things so that in Christ you might be all in all.

Amen.

MARCH 2

Certain you are here

O Lord My God:

Open to your love, I feel you teaching me today through the simple movements of my daily life and especially through my resting prayer in your presence.

Certain you are here, I trust that all things today will work together for my good.

Amen.

MARCH 3

All is well

God of Tender Mercy:

Sometimes I am tempted to close down in fear and frustration. In that moment, I give thanks for your tender mercy assuring me that all is well. You are here.

Amen.

MARCH 4

The silence in which you meet me

God Who Waits:

I return to my center today, finding abundant life in you.

Resting there, I am awakened to the gift of my being and becoming in your presence.

I offer my being and becoming as a song for the silence in which you meet me with your living Word.

Amen.

MARCH 5

Caught in the mystery of this life

God of Love and Light:

During these days may you—

Light the lamp of my eyes with wisdom.

Light the torch of my heart with love.

Cure my sadness.

Warm my coldness.

Drench my inner drought with your divine love.

Lead me into the abandonment of your loving embrace.

Caught in the mystery of this life, I am upheld by the experience of your love in the silence.

Through Christ, with Christ, in the unity of the Spirit.

Amen.

* * *

MARCH 6

Set my heart to sail deeper into your love

Eternal and Loving God:

I am filled with a sweetness that rises into my heart with song. Perhaps it is the feeling of love. Ancient melodies remind me of an untold freedom, long lost, awaiting me. Shall I finally believe it and set my heart to sail deeper into your love?

Amen.

MARCH 7

The only wound that need not ever heal

Abba:

Quicken in me the presence of your living Word, through which I receive the wound of love so to ponder the beauty and grace of all things created.

Your wound humbles me to tears, not so much in pain, but in the joy of your mercy. This is the only wound that need not ever heal, whose symbol is the cross and whose image is your descending dove.

Amen.

MARCH 8

What needs to be forgiven, healed, and celebrated

Giver of Life and Love:

Embrace me with mercy and grace. You know what is stored within my heart. You know the issues in my tissues. You know what needs to be forgiven, healed, and celebrated.

Strengthen me in the silence and teach me in the light of your love.

Amen.

■ ■ ■

MARCH 9

The uprising of your energy

God of Transformation:

Help me feel again the uprising of your energy meeting me in the furnace of my being—awakening, empowering, driving me by your Spirit further into the wilderness to confront the deepest layers of my hidden false-self and programs for happiness that cannot possibly work.

Amen.

■ ■ ■

MARCH 10

Upheld in the light of your resurrection

Strength of My Life:

I am promised that there is a stream by which I may grow in every season, flowing with living water available for my flourishing if I drink it day and night. Yet, I am hindered in doing so by distractions and undisciplined habits.

Sometimes it seems impossible such growth could ever happen in me.

Help me, Lord. I wish to walk with joy, upheld in the light of your resurrection.

Amen.

MARCH 11

With me in suffering and shock

God My Father and Mother:

You are here with me in suffering and shock.

Have mercy and help. As the world spins, draw my attention

to the center of my life. My hope for all who are suffering right now is your presence of the living-whole, who binds the broken parts together with resurrection power.

Amen.

MARCH 12

The great mystery of Christ

God of My Lifetime:

Protect me from the temptations of the world and the errors of the false self. Fill my heart and body with the strength of the Holy Spirit, and illumine my mind with the knowledge of the great mystery of Christ.

Amen.

MARCH 13

Unlock the mystery of life

God of My Lifetime:

What is the formula to unlock the mystery of life? I surrender the life I call my own and discover it anew as a sheer gift. I am therefore free from the need to hold on to this thing called my "self," released to live by faith.

Amen.

MARCH 14

Your vision for my becoming

Silent Love, Source of Life:

Prompt me into your possibilities, and strengthen me through failures.

I release all my thoughts and feelings of accusation and guilt and receive the gift of freedom in your long-suffering love.

I consent to your work of renovation and trust your vision

for my becoming, rather than my addiction to what I have been.

Amen.

■ ■ ■

MARCH 15

Turn my Lazarus life into resurrection love

Heart of Love:

Turn my Lazarus life into resurrection love. Use the failures of my best efforts as the locations of your transforming grace. In my powerlessness to do, draw me into deeper union with you.

Amen.

■ ■ ■

MARCH 16

The ashen mark upon my forehead

Spirit of God:

The ashen mark upon my forehead, now washed clean, remains in my heart as a symbol of my emptiness and my need for you.

Hungry, I can be fed.

Empty, I can be filled.

Barren, I can give birth.

And what is feeding, filling, and birthing in me but the incarnation of love itself?

This is the unyielding power of Jesus Christ birthing in me something new.

Amen.

MARCH 17
Everything is useful for transformation

Indwelling Presence:

With the confidence of your love and goodness, reveal my self-serving tendencies so as to free me to become truly generous in love. I consent to your interior healing today, assured that in Christ everything is useful for my transformation.

Amen.

MARCH 18
Eternity lingers deeper

Beloved:

I wait. I pray. Give me strength to endure this Lenten fast and help me with the sneaky temptations I don't expect.

Underneath my hunger, the taste of eternity lingers deeper than any satisfaction food might provide.

Amen.

MARCH 19

Become more silently beautiful

Creator and Healer:

Awaken me to make amends to those I have wronged. Bring your life-creating power to my broken relationships and your healing grace to all enduring wounds.

Amen.

MARCH 20

Fear no longer holds me

Living Presence:

I am abandoned unto you.

You are my strength.

You are my foundation.

I call upon you and am helped.

Fear no longer holds me. You do. And you are love.

Amen.

MARCH 21

The shadow hope of resurrection cresting near

Divine Love, Silent Presence:

Descending with Jesus into the remembrance of his Passion past, I look ahead to the shadow hope of resurrection cresting near, beneath any crosses I bear.

Explanations and justifications all pale to the color of pain I see among humankind. Strangely, I am comforted seeing that your resurrection light also contains all the hues of the human condition, including the color of our tears, violence, and suffering.

Amen.

■ ■ ■

MARCH 22

Stand in wonder as you surrender to the violent depths

Lord Jesus, Living Christ:

Prepare me to be with you in the center of Jerusalem in my worshipful heart. Gather me in the upper room of my mind to meet with you in devotion and friendship. I am ready to receive you. I steel my heart to stand in wonder as you surrender to the violent depths of the human condition for my rescue and healing.

Amen.

■ ■ ■

MARCH 23

Turn my demands into preferences

O God My Healer:

Turn my demands into preferences,

and my preferences into detachment,

and detachment into pure love,

and love into union,

consummating into only oneness so that there is no other—

to be judged, demanded, or preferred.

Amen.

MARCH 24

A bad case of the human condition

Holy Spirit:

Your quiet fire purifies me to the depths with a subtle love so powerful I begin to recognize that I have come from you at the same time I become aware I have strayed, spending energy pursuing programs for my own happiness rather than listening to your love.

I confess I have a bad case of the human condition. But you have the perfect remedy. In the silence, your healing unfolds, one layer after another, until Christ is unbound and revealed risen in and through me and all who cry out for help in simple faith.

Amen.

MARCH 25

Release my demands for my life to be different

Jesus Christ, My Life:

You have shown me the way of surrender. Help me release the demands for my life to be different. In total gratitude, I wish to accept life as it occurs today, neither thinking I deserve more nor feeling guilty for all I have been given. I rest in humility recognizing that all things work together for my transformation in and through you.

Amen.

MARCH 26

The swift light of conscious love

Lord Jesus, Living Christ:

May the swift light of conscious love lift my life through any weariness loading me down.

May the lightness of your love uphold me amidst any sinking feelings of guilt, shame, or depression.

May the wind shear of grace propel me quickly through the cold choices that lead nowhere.

Amen.

■ ■ ■

MARCH 27

Love becomes union

Uncircled Light, Unbounded Love:

I wish to speak of my gratitude, yet I cannot say what I wish to say.

Your love overwhelms me.

Sometimes silence is saying enough.

In and through Christ I live, move, and have all my saying and unsaying.

Amen.

■ ■ ■

MARCH 28

The way into the mystery

God of Peace:

Grant me the grace to meet each thing, event, and relationship I perceive as a problem today with a deepened attention to the center that holds all things together with an intelligence that transcends my perceptions.

Where I feel friction with others, reveal the way into the mystery of seeing how your love connects the many ways of being and the multiple points of human perspective, all with perfect harmony.

Amen.

■ ■ ■

MARCH 29

Surrender to your presence

Holy Spirit:

Let the fire of your abiding love cleanse my heart, forging my will to surrender to your presence and action, transforming me from one degree of glory to the next.

Draw me to you. Gift me with faithful companions who support my intentions to follow the way despite the competing allurements and alternative paths and programs for happiness that tempt me to neglect my recent deepest intentions.

Amen.

MARCH 30

Your Word is the occurrence of total self-giving love

Holy Spirit of God:

Beyond comparison, beyond despair, beyond every heart, mind, and body care—

Your guiding, encircling love connects me to the truth so easily hidden by structures of power, control, and wealth.

The truth is that this world emanates from your Word and your Word is the occurrence of total self-giving love.

Amen.

MARCH 31

A world in process of being reborn

Living and Radiant Source of Love:

Awaken me to the importance of wisely using my time to prepare a reservoir of interior peace.

Show me how to identity with common human difficulties through fasting, prayer, and almsgiving and to realize that my own problems do not define me, but can connect me through empathy to a world in process of being reborn.

Amen.

APRIL

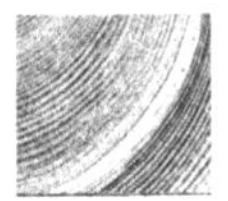

It is as if God says to me:

With simple acceptance of my Triune mystery, join with the community of saints to remember my promises.

During this month of new life through death, please know, feel, and remember how hope comes close in the depths, bringing my Son's light, life, and love.

APRIL 1

You are the shadow that crosses near in the silence

Living God:

You are the center of the cosmos and the summation of all that has ever been said.

You are the awakening that warms the world.

You are the living connection holding me close in my seasons of separation.

You are the source of oneness binding the earth and its people to our unseen foundation and emerging destiny.

You are the shadow that crosses near in the silence of prayer.

Amen.

APRIL 2

To the depths of outer darkness

Lord Jesus:

Thank you for showing me the way, the truth, and the life to the Father. Thank you for returning me to the Father through your life, suffering, and death.

You who went all the way down into the human condition and beyond to the depths of outer darkness can return and rescue me all the way up to God and the heights of eternal light. Perhaps this is the moment the word *hallelujah* was born.

Amen.

APRIL 3

The chalice of your silent love

O God Beyond My Comprehension:

I drink the water of liquid faith, poured from the chalice of your silent love. My secret name is etched forever in the book of life, and I receive this heralded victory like a promise of love sealed with your Gethsemane tears.

Amen.

APRIL 4

A more complete child of God

Beloved Jesus Christ:

Under your mercy, failures become my best teacher, showing me how to live more freely in your love. Through your resurrection, ward off the harmful influences and experiences of life. Give your living water and bread of life so that I may become a more complete child of God, not just a servant of life.

Amen.

■ ■ ■

APRIL 5

Draw me into the love that unites

Beloved Source of Life:

I wish to feel your risen power in the center of my heart. Let this Easter season be for melting my inner ice blocks into living water. Soften the preferences that separate and draw me into the love that unites.

In this practical work, I am held by Christ, whose cross and tomb are symbols of your invitation to a different kind of life. I choose surrender of self so as to receive resurrection to life.

Amen.

■ ■ ■

APRIL 6

Transform my patterns of judgment

Heavenly Father:

Transform my patterns of judgment into abounding grace. Heal the pain in me that restricts the freedom of your love and of Christ's resurrection. Let me see the fruit of peace.

Amen.

■ ■ ■

APRIL 7

Seeking and knocking

Divine Healer:

I'm asking, seeking, and knocking to know and experience more of your will for my life and the power of your right-now-ever-sustaining love.

Amen.

APRIL 8

A temple of truth

Beloved:

Teach me the truth of your reality in my ordinary experiences. I consent to your point of view and wish to cease being my own fixed point of reference.

You are the life I long for yet resist in my attempts to find life everywhere else. Gently transform me into a temple of truth in union with Jesus Christ by the power of your Holy Spirit.

Amen.

APRIL 9

More than I can ask or imagine

Abba:

Open me with the gentleness of your love.

I see that I have room to grow and request the insights necessary to surrender more completely even without complete understanding.

You are bringing about in me something more than I can ask or imagine. Give me patience as you hold me while I grow.

I affirm that your presence is sufficient for all situations that I encounter on this unfolding journey.

Amen.

■ ■ ■

APRIL 10

My deepest truth in the face of life's deepest darkness

Lord Jesus, Living Christ:

You are the answer to my deepest questions.

You are my stability in all my uncertainty.

You are provision to all my needs.

Your love dwells with me in the temple of my heart and mind.

In you, there is nothing that can separate me from God.

With these prayerful intentions, I declare my deepest truth in the face of life's deepest darkness. I challenge the shadows of doubt, depression, anger, fear, and judgment with the light of resurrection love.

Amen.

APRIL 11

Depths of your life and heights of your love

Living God of Life and Love:

I aim to order my days by the inner awareness of heaven and my moments by the in-breath of Spirit through Word and sacrament.

Reveal the mystery of Christ to me in personal and profound ways.

Help me see the depths of your life and heights of your love beyond my judgments, perceptions, and false self motivations.

Amen.

APRIL 12

Your abundance of grace

Lord Jesus, Living Christ:

Your multi-chance love extends deeper than all my failures. It extends, over and again, as practical grace uplifting, helping, sustaining, providing in every moment of my life.

Just when I thought I could not or do not have what it will take, you invite me to trust you and cast my net into your abundance of grace.

Amen.

APRIL 13

Defined by your love

Heart of My Heart:

Remind me again in the silence of prayerful surrender that I cannot explain my own existence. Life is a gift.

I am not defined by my situations. I am defined by your love. Enlarge me for prayer. Just because I can't see the stars in the daylight does not mean they are not there. I am like that; always in you and you in me, despite appearances in life to the contrary. Today, I remember: Christ in me, the hope of glory.

Amen.

APRIL 14

Through the places of my brokenness

Ministering Spirit of God:

Help me remember that I come from you and return to you, and in between I am invited to grow in love. I wish to feel your grace attending to me through the places of my brokenness, inviting me deeper into your love.

Amen.

APRIL 15

Deepen my understanding

Abba:

Deepen my understanding so that I do not drift in the mist of doubt or miss the mark of your living truth. Bring me to new life in an ever-flourishing relationship with your Son, my shepherd, Jesus Christ.

Amen.

APRIL 16

Thank you

Most Holy and Loving God:

Thank you today for the gift of life.

Thank you for awakening me to your abundant life.

Help me to see you in the midst of all my day-to-day living.

Amen.

APRIL 17

Your movements of beauty

Lord Jesus, Living Christ:

As I begin a new day in this resurrection season, I request an attentive heart. Despite the busy days, help me to stop and listen for your movements. Startle me with your beauty and goodness hiding in plain sight.

Amen.

APRIL 18

Amongst brighter beings

Holy Trinity of Light, Life, and Love:

Draw me into spiritual community with you and with others. Deepen my spiritual friendships and draw me amongst brighter beings in whose company I might feel understood and whose common aims and interests will be a help to my journey.

I recognize and request this need for my own life and agree to try and do the same in the lives of others where needed. Respond and surprise me with your provision.

Amen.

APRIL 19

Support my intentions

Holy Spirit:

Draw me to you on this one-way journey to the heart of our Father in Christ the Son.

Gift me with faithful companions who support my intentions to follow this way despite all the competing allurements and alternative paths promising happiness.

Amen.

APRIL 20

Lighthearted joy raising me up

Lord Jesus:

Gently release me from my personal agendas and impulsive actions so that I might live more completely under the certainty of your leading, guiding, and teaching.

As you do, fill my heart with lighthearted joy, raising me up from the heaviness of gloom.

Amen.

APRIL 21

Your love in me and my life in you

Abba:

I rest in your continued anointing.

Guide my intellect to clearly see.

Guide my will to harmoniously choose.

Open my heart to feel your love in me and my life in you.

Amen.

APRIL 22

I am a part of this living Word from the beginning

Source of All Life:

Your Word sustains all life and brings order amidst the chaos. I am part of this living Word from the beginning. Today, I say "yes" to your wish for the flourishing of the creation. Through prayer and action, I agree to play my part so that the will of heaven may be more present here on earth.

Amen.

APRIL 23

I cast myself upon your goodness

Beloved of My Heart:

Today, I cast myself upon your goodness.

Words fail to describe the joy of my salvation.

You meet me in my despair.

You heal me in my brokenness.

You anoint me in my surrender.

Amen.

APRIL 24

The healing my body needs

God My Healer:

In the certainty that you can bring the healing my body needs to become the fullness of what is possible as a co-heir with Christ, I surrender to you.

Amen.

APRIL 25

The path I am to take

Threefold Holy One:

I try to pass courageously through life situations, challenges, temptations, and conflicts, requesting wisdom to make decisions according to the inspiration of your self-giving love, rather than the constrictions of my demands.

Reveal in clear ways the path I am to take today. Help me stay open to your love and awake to your presence in each person and every situation I encounter.

Amen.

APRIL 26

You are the miracle

Lord Jesus, Eternal Christ:

I make my claim on reality requesting—

forgiveness of every debt,

provision for every need,

strength for every weakness,

comfort for every trouble,

healing for every sickness,

peace for every anxiety,

joy for every sorrow,

light for every darkness,

love for every longing,

companionship for every loneliness,

presence for every absence,

meaning for every emptiness,

bread for every hunger,

water for every thirst,

shelter for every storm,

and abundance for every lack.

You are the miracle.

You part the waters again and again, inviting humankind to ask, seek, and knock.

I await your whisper in the silence and envision your Word bringing everything to life.

Amen.

APRIL 27

That my words may be life-giving

Lord Jesus, Living Christ:

Speak into my life and unbind the love waiting to be born in me. Radiate your life into my heart that my words may be life-giving and my countenance joy-reflecting.

Amen.

APRIL 28

The house of wisdom

Spirit of Truth and Goodness:

The wisdom of God is infinite and unfathomable, yet it becomes utterly personal when I ask for help. I surrender to you the impulses to live by my own wisdom. In this quiet moment, I request that your house of wisdom might be opened to me more today than before.

Amen.

APRIL 29

Your name is a treatment

Holy One:

Your very name is a treatment for my body and soul. I speak it softly as my affirmation of your healing help in the spaces of my life.

Your name is a shield of light, a midnight sun blazing in the darkness of my unconscious choices and behavior.

Your name is a song of love wooing me into heartfulness and the possibilities of harmony.

Your name is a blue spring morning triumphing with the power of new life made green through the darkness.

I search my heart and find the silence and the Spirit who teaches me to say, "Hallowed be thy name."

Amen.

APRIL 30

Loosen the webs

Almighty God:

Loosen the webs that entangle my heart and prevent the reception of your faithful love.

Prepare my life for the fullness of your presence.

Renewed through prayer today, I let go into the vastness of your depths and the vitality of your Word.

Amen.

MAY

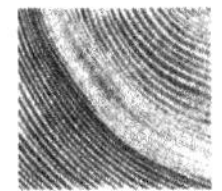

It is as if God says to me:

This moment, right now, is alive with the possibility to surrender to my salvation. I can free you to live in love toward all, even when you are tempted to respond with less than love, forgiveness, or kindness.

With the full bloom of spring, remember that I wish for your flourishing. I invite you into fruitfulness in every relationship, and especially with me. I am with you, helping you to always reach an inner abundance, especially now.

MAY 1

Hold me in your steadfast love

Faithful Giver of Life:

Let your face shine on me. Hold me in your steadfast love. Let me know your forgiveness, for I call upon you. Let all my fears be cast out. Let me speak with the integrity of truth.

Amen.

MAY 2

Pour out your Spirit

Divine Love:

Pour out your Spirit upon me that I might know and experience your presence, so that even on my worst day I have the certitude that you are bringing about my intended destiny.

Amen.

MAY 3

Keep me aware

Spirit of God:

Guide my choices today so that what I say and do corresponds to the truth of my union in Christ with you. While I go about my duties of the day, keep me aware and connected to the hidden source of your love, claiming me as a beloved despite my fickle faith.

Amen.

MAY 4

Your presence undergirding

Lord Jesus Christ:

Speak to me in the strength of your love so that I might surrender more of myself to you and recognize your presence undergirding every dimension and moment of my life.

Forgive my attempts to take control and live as if you are not ultimate reality bringing blessings beyond my limited perception.

Thank you for the inability to explain my own existence. Help me see how the suffering of this life is just the right place for me to surrender to your strength that holds all things together.

Amen.

MAY 5

The assurance of things unseen

God of Perfect Provision:

For every fear I have of not being understood, and for every hope I fear will not be fulfilled, remind me that you bring about unexpected gifts with the power to change everything and bless me beyond what I could ever ask or imagine.

Amen.

MAY 6

The rhythm of rest

God of Perfect Peace:

Give me the patience to wait for your best gifts in a world moving fast.

Draw me into the rhythm of rest that my body needs and the goodness of relationships that my heart craves.

While the world is unpredictable, reveal your life-giving presence permanently available in the silence.

Amen.

MAY 7

When I feel tempted

Ever Faithful One:

When I feel tempted to give up on love, please restore, replenish, encourage, uphold, sustain, empower, and provide all that is required for me to endure.

Amen.

MAY 8

The moment I was born

Everlasting Giver of Life:

There is a truth in me that shines despite its hiddenness. This truth was given the moment I was born. It is my identity, which comes from you. Whatever my boss or colleagues or family members or spouse or friends think they see when they look at me, there is more.

I stand in the knowledge of my deepest being today, with perfect assurance that nothing can separate me from your love in Christ.

Amen.

MAY 9

To simply be

Abba:

Free me from the compulsion to do, get, or keep up appearances. Give me the courage to simply be and belong to you. Help me see your path to freedom when I am tempted to buy my way to what I think is happiness. Fill me again with the joys of life in Christ.

Amen.

■ ■ ■

MAY 10

Sustaining comfort

Lord Jesus, Living Christ:

Touch me with the sustaining comfort necessary to thrive throughout the demands of this day. Seal me from overreactions that deplete my force for love, and fill me with the insights for dealing with difficult decisions and perplexing relationships.

Amen.

■ ■ ■

MAY 11

You are the gift

Spirit of God:

You are the gift my soul has been waiting for in the silence and throughout all the seasons of my life—even when I didn't know it.

Plant your Word in my heart and birth your wisdom through me in ways I can't begin to comprehend, to bless others through counsel, friendship, and a joyful countenance.

Amen.

■ ■ ■

MAY 12

Turn me into a temple of light

Beloved Abba:

I celebrate the drenching of your Spirit for the destiny of love and begin today saying "yes" to you, stepping back from myself to create a space for your grace to fill.

I will surrender to silence and consent to your holy presence and action.

Through this time of simple prayer, continue to transform my body into a temple of your light, life, and love.

Amen.

■ ■ ■

MAY 13

Nurture wholeness

Most Gracious and Loving God:

As I rest with you in prayer, I request the mind of Christ. Guide my decisions. Instruct my conversations. Nurture wholeness in my relationships.

In this moment, fill me with the awareness that in Christ by your Spirit I belong to you.

Amen.

■ ■ ■

MAY 14

Sink deeply into the silence

Beloved:

I wish to sink deeply into the silence and receive your life-giving rest.

For all the demands upon me, for all the people who need my time and attention, for all the situations that require my best efforts, I request help.

Thank you for the ways your grace releases me from having to perform and liberates me to live freely in each moment—gently, lightly, calmly.

Amen.

MAY 15

Remind me

Lord Jesus Christ:

Anoint me with your Spirit so I can speak in love and act in truth.

Where I lack clarity, reveal your will.

Where I presume to know, teach me simple trust.

Where I am impatient, remind me of your timelessness.

Amen.

■ ■ ■

MAY 16

The impossible is possible

Lord Jesus, Living Christ:

In your grace the impossible is possible.

Awaken me to see this truth more clearly, especially when I am tempted to forget and believe the lie that everything depends upon me.

Amen.

■ ■ ■

MAY 17

Mercy nourishing growth

Abba:

I often taste the bitterness of judgment and criticism. Help me to feel my innocence in your mercy. Replace my narratives of blame, guilt, and shame with a melody of forgiveness.

Then, loosen the knots of judgment I tie around others, so that I too might forgive and feel your mercy nourishing growth.

Amen.

MAY 18

The everlasting highway of saints

Love Beyond All Love:

By your mercy, I am here on earth to receive and reflect your glory as a vessel of Christ.

By your grace, I am one mile of the everlasting highway of saints encircled in the light of prayer and worship destined for the city of God.

Amen.

MAY 19

In between I learn to love

Life-giving Holy Trinity:

Thank you for the gift of the human journey.

Help me use this lifetime to become love.

Amen.

MAY 20

The realm of your Spirit

Sky-Rending Fire of Love:

Everything I am experiencing today is connected to the reality of your love, even if I can't figure out how.

May the realm of your Spirit continuously uphold the destiny of humankind and lead me to personally experience and receive more fully the reality of Jesus Christ in sacrament and silence.

Amen.

MAY 21

The calm whisper of your Spirit

Light upon Light:

Since I do not know what this day will bring, I ask for indications of providence and guidance for my spiritual journey.

Open the ear of my soul to hear the calm whisper of your Spirit speaking directly to my heart and to believe again the ancient promises from above.

Open the eyes of my heart so as to see with the certainty of faith in the light of your loving purpose.

Amen.

■ ■ ■

MAY 22

Unveiling my falseness with love

Lord Jesus My Teacher:

You are my teacher. Unveil my falseness with your love. Help me see that there is nothing I need to hide from you.

Heal the intentions of my heart so I can love and serve with freedom and generosity.

Amen.

■ ■ ■

MAY 23

See beyond the surface

Living God of Life and Love:

Help me see beyond the surface of my external judgments, superficial perceptions, and selfish pharisaical motivations.

Turn me more into love.

Amen.

■ ■ ■

MAY 24

Your graceful way among us

Lord of the Universe:

I lift my voice in prayer with the chorus of the cosmos, grateful to be here witnessing your graceful way among us.

Your name is sung in praise by light.

May your wisdom flourish here on earth.

Amen.

MAY 25

Conveying fearless joy

Eternal Stillness, Expanding Love:

Speak to my heart in the silence and let your Word take shape in the solitude of my prayer, bringing increased joy and peace in my social interactions today.

Amen.

MAY 26

Your Spirit loves to work in the secret places of shame

God of Hope Who Moves Beyond Human Limits:

Give me strength to come face to face with my false ways. Jolt me with a vision of what my future can be in you.

Your Spirit loves to work in the secret places of shame and with my wounded memories accumulated over a lifetime.

Therefore, I ask for a quality of life manifesting the stability of wisdom and the fecundity of love.

In the name that is the highest power, my greatest joy, my deepest truth, and my strongest hope: the savior anointed, Jesus the Christ.

Amen.

MAY 27

Seek the higher things of life and love

Abba:

Empower me today with a renewed force of will to know the fullness of your truth available to humankind.

I wish to feel the guidance of higher influences awakening me to the experience of your presence beyond and underneath the fears and demands of my surface personality and worldly interactions.

Draw me into your depth, which is also the height and breadth of the knowlege of your love in Christ.

Amen.

MAY 28

You write new stories with old sentences

Unending Word of Life:

You write new stories with old sentences.

You transform deep hurts into sources of love.

You are the one I seek in all my pursuits.

Hold me as I weep, and whisper strength when everything seems to be falling apart.

You are here with me.

In this moment, that is more than enough.

Amen.

MAY 29

Deepen this ancient belonging

Holy Spirit of God:

Connect me to the growing source that keeps me strong even when my body feels weak.

Nurture me through the flow of wisdom descending upon me over the years from lessons learned and passages read.

And I will praise you this day for the ways your playfulness keeps me grounded, your wisdom keeps me focused, and your intention keeps me moving into the mystery of your love for others. Deepen this ancient belonging, and take me into eternity.

Amen.

MAY 30

Start in me

O God, My God:

Do not forsake your world and its nations.

May your Spirit of peace bring an end to all violence and war.

Start in me.

Amen.

MAY 31

Stimulate my sense of wonder

God of Creation:

Stimulate my sense of wonder to marvel at the existence of the universe and my place in it as a spiritual being in development through this embodied experience.

Help me feel your transforming and available love coming down through the ray of creation, calling me to more harmonious ways of thinking, feeling, and doing.

Amen.

JUNE

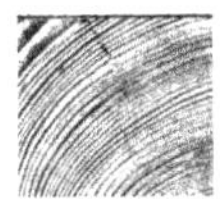

It is as if God says to me:

My love moves with the cadence of the earth, waltzing around the sun.

Soon I am bringing the light to full, to remind you how I am also the light of the world.

Watch for me. I will shine into your life with love.

JUNE 1

Awaken me with your gentle light

Abba:

Pour out your Spirit upon my broken dreams and awaken me with your gentle light of love into the realization of your presence in my life today.

Amen.

JUNE 2

Your connecting presence everywhere

Transforming Presence:

Awaken me in the silence of prayer so I might perceive, relate, and respond to you, to myself, to others, and to the creation with increasing awareness to your connecting presence everywhere through Christ by the Spirit.

Amen.

JUNE 3

More fully share in your life

Abba:

Lead me into the living water of Scripture and replenish me with your written Word so that I may more fully share in your life with peace, wisdom, and mindfulness.

Amen.

JUNE 4

Incongruency is occurring

Source of the Creation:

Incongruency is occurring on this planet between reality and the ideal. I am indeed fallen from the peace of paradise. Today I request the transforming grace that spans the space between what is and what might be. May I play my part well in the balance of your Holy Spirit.

Amen.

JUNE 5

I turn my heart toward your resurrection

Beloved:

I enter into silence each morning and night like a spider spins its web by the light, catching nourishment in the solitude of its spindle threads.

I turn my heart toward your resurrection like the sunflowers spinning their golden heads to drink the light of day. It seems life is more alive on these June mornings as summertime unleashes its impulse to thrive.

My heart joins with the greening lushness wishing for the fullness of who I can become. What fruition will appear in the darkness? What can the light of your love do in me?

I wait for you in the secret silence only to discover in my life the dew of your presence. You've been here all along, hidden by the turning horizon now revealing your life in me.

Amen.

JUNE 6

Your stream carves into my heart's darkness

Living God:

Your Spirit arrives as a morning rain, showing up like a surprise guest. Listening to her voice at my heart's doorway, I discover her name is Love, "but friends call me Mercy," she adds quickly.

She reaches toward me, cupped hands dripping holy water. "I can heal you," she says, shyly, looking into my eyes. "See, taste this..." And I drink from her vessel.

O lady of life and love:

Your stream carves into my heart's darkness, and the light seeps in.

Amen.

JUNE 7

You are the key that unlocks the mystery

Lord Jesus Christ:

You are the key that unlocks the mystery that is called existence.

You are the Word that speaks in the silence that is, was, and always shall be.

You are the presence that pulses in the vastness attending to even the imperfect me.

You are the life that vivifies the planet in the blood and bread of common things.

You are the one and the many in whom I return to the Father, existence itself in loving communion with all beings and becomings.

Amen.

JUNE 8

The presence of your healing love

God of My Prayers:

Bless me with the presence of your healing love felt in the silence of my inner room.

I feel you calling to me. It's as if you are saying to my heart, "I wish to speak face to face with you in silent, wordless wonder."

Why do I resist?

O silent love, I consent to your Triune threefold presence, beloved creator, redeemer, and sustainer.

Amen.

JUNE 9

The power of your protection in love

God of My Life:

Flow through my body today that I might know the joy of your creating;

the certainty of your presence;

the power of your protection;

and the fullness of your joy.

Amen.

JUNE 10

Breaking the bonds of suffering

Beloved Beyond Boundaries:

I lift up my heart for the poor, the kidnapped, the forsaken, the alone, the tortured, the abused, the hospitalized, the falsely accused, the hungry, the wounded souls of our world.

In the prayer of my heart, I request a different future, breaking the bonds of suffering, bringing healing and wholeness in the name of Christ.

Amen.

JUNE 11

Your grace works

Abba:

Your presence underneath the noise of the demands of daily life fills my heart with peace.

Your Word cleanses negative emotions that I don't know how to stop on my own.

Your grace works in my inner room of silent prayer, taking away jealousies, hatreds, vanities, pride, and prejudices that hinder consciously chosen love.

Thank you for your healing grace.

Amen.

JUNE 12

You hold me while I grow

Beloved Source of Security:

I wish for total freedom from all forms of destructive fear.

In its place, lead me into the freedom of surrender.

You hold me while I grow, and in this confidence I release anxieties about my life—its survival and success—and trust you with my unfolding story.

Amen.

JUNE 13

Worthy of love

Beloved Source of Love:

Assure me in the depth of my being just how worthy of love I am on your generous terms.

Renew my thinking in light of this truth so that all my actions are guided by a sense of contentment, not envy.

Amen.

JUNE 14

Lead me deeper

Beloved One in Three:

Lead me deeper into the mystery of your love. Help me feel your presence in my weaknesses and all my wanderings.

Amen.

JUNE 15

Who I may become in your grace

Giver of Every Good Gift:

Help me see who I truly am beneath the masks of my making, and who I may become in your grace.

I pray in your most holy threefold name: Father, Son, and Holy Spirit.

Amen.

JUNE 16

Make me meek in the shadow of your glory

God of Gentle Power:

Make me meek in the shadow of your glory, to better reflect your love and truth. Help me remember that I live and move and have my being in Christ.

Amen.

JUNE 17

Fill my poverty with your fullness

Heart of My Heart:

Let me see you. Let me feel you. Let me know you. Let me love you.

Fill my poverty with your completeness.

Satisfy my hunger and thirst with your integrating truth that leads to life.

In Christ, the mystery of your love for all.

Amen.

JUNE 18

A school of love

Spirit of Christ:

Thank you for this day and for every opportunity I have and will experience. I wish it all for my development in being and growth in love, goodness, and wisdom. Mediate each misunderstanding I experience with another that my relationships may become a school of love.

Amen.

JUNE 19

I wait for your first move in the darkness of surrender

Living Presence, Silent Love:

I wait for your first move in the darkness of surrender, lifting me into joy.

Whatever else may happen today, you are my center and source, blinding light, burning love, blooming life.

Amen.

JUNE 20

The awareness needed to choose the highest good

Spirit of God:

Activate in me the awareness needed to choose the highest good and to avoid that which leads to suffering, for my own life or for anyone else.

Amen.

JUNE 21

Fill me with your living Word of love

Abba:

On this day in celebration of the fullness of sunlight, anoint me with your peace so that I might become a peacemaker.

Fill me with your living Word of love so that I might decrease in judgment and increase in total grace through Christ by your Spirit.

Amen.

JUNE 22

Your leading in the silence

Living God of Love:

Give me ears to hear your request beneath the demands of this moment.

I wish to listen for your leading in the silence.

Help me listen beyond the stories I spin about others and my own self. Your leading is clear in the silence: "Love one another because you are one in me."

Amen.

■ ■ ■

JUNE 23

The joy that can only arrive through love

Beloved Jesus Christ:

Pour out your Spirit upon me so I can more completely love my family. Strengthen me to work for the freedom that can only come through forgiveness and the joy that can only arrive through love.

Amen.

JUNE 24

Inspire me with your spiritual love

Beloved Mother of Jesus:

Inspire me with your spiritual love so that I might be released more from my false-self into the freedom of your beloved Son, Christ in me.

Amen.

JUNE 25

Love saturates the empty space

You Who Dwell in the Temple of My Heart:

Sweeten me in the silence as your Word of love saturates the empty space between the thoughts where grace can grow with speed and strength.

Do the one thing necessary in me that can't be undone by life or luck.

Make me more yours than my own until all there is, *is* Christ.

Amen.

JUNE 26

Abide with me even while all of life is occurring

Lord Jesus Christ:

Awaken me by the touch of your Spirit to the presence of your closeness in each and every moment of my life.

Give me the courage I need to do what I have been asked to do.

Show me how to separate from the fearful thoughts and feelings that occur in response to all of life's demands.

Draw me deeper into your love and abide with me even while all of life is occurring.

Amen.

JUNE 27

The miracle of many voices becoming one

Jesus Christ:

Refresh me by your Spirit.

Lead me into peace and understanding with others and help me experience the miracle of many voices becoming one in you.

Amen.

JUNE 28

Strengthen and sustain me

Almighty God:

May the healing power flowing from the fountain-heart of Jesus Christ strengthen and sustain me with every consolation by his Word and Spirit.

Amen.

JUNE 29

Let me hear the sacred names of God

Silent Giver of Life:

Let me hear the sacred names of God in the firmament of silence surrounding the earth and cosmos, from before time in the wordless Word that forms my being and all things.

You are made visible in the flourish of petals glowing orange in mid-summer heat; in the trickle of glacier melt watering the steep slopes, birthing life downstream.

O God, I name your wordless name in handfuls of this living earth, holy and bound to you from deep seas to high mountain heaps.

I name to revere, not conquer; to cherish, not exploit.

Named in me, in you, in him and her, in this and that, in all things poured out in order to pour back to you.

Amen.

JUNE 30

To you, my Good Shepherd, I give my elemental being

To you, my Good Shepherd, I give my elemental being and all inner shadows that rise in opposition to love.

Use this day as my teacher.

Reveal where there is interior resistance to your truth and transformation, and bring the joyful release of feeling forgiven in each moment when I remember who I am and what you wish for me to become.

Amen.

JULY

It is as if God says to me:

You are a lamp and my love is your fuel.

I love you and wish to anoint your life with the kind of light that heals your deepest darkness.

I am with you on your journey.

Follow the Son who knows the way and is always close.

JULY 1

The space for grace

Beloved Giver of Life:

When thoughts occur that lead to discouragement, give me the grace to not believe my own negativity.

Let the mind of Christ fill my thinking with praise, gratitude, and joy.

Amen.

JULY 2

Where miracles occur

Abba:

Lead me into the abiding place where miracles occur in the silence of your love, beyond all understanding.

In Christ, with Christ, for Christ I pray.

Amen.

JULY 3

The encompassing of God

Eternal Now, Unending Center:

The encompassing of God be upon my form and upon my frame.

The encompassing of divine love and the grace of the Trinity be upon me eternally, shielding me from hate, from harm, and from all ill.

Amen.

JULY 4

Reveal the way of gentle love

God Beyond All Descriptions:

Show me the path through my pride and reveal the way of gentle love when I feel inflated with self-admiration.

I speak this prayer through Christ, who is the way, the truth, and the life, and my destination.

Amen.

JULY 5

Set apart for the destiny of love

God of Perfect Holiness and Love:

Pour out your Spirit upon me and complete the renovation of my heart into a mansion of love.

I am an ordinary peasant waking each morning looking for bread.

I know that there is nowhere I need to go, for you are already here.

I see that there is nothing I need, for you have already given me everything by giving me yourself.

Amen.

JULY 6

A Magdalene moment of stunning certitude

Lord Jesus, Living Christ:

I wish to hear and feel your voice of love descending upon me in the mysteries of sacrament and silence.

When I cannot see or recognize you in the form and field of my day-to-day vision, surprise me with a Magdalene moment of stunning certitude.

Amen.

JULY 7

A Stephen moment of surrender

Lord Jesus, Risen Christ:

As I face the presence of pain and suffering in my life, speak my name in silence. Lead me to a Stephen moment of surrender, inspired by visions of my future in and through your love.

Amen.

JULY 8

The home of my heart

Beloved Christ, Close and Silent:

I offer myself this day as a location through which your love can flow.

Let it be in me according to your Word.

May your grace flow in and through me today.

Amen.

JULY 9

Your presence changes everything

Abba:

Nourish me with your love so that whatever is occurring in this life might be received with gratitude, recognizing that your presence changes everything.

Amen.

JULY 10

Help me listen

God of Mercy and Grace:

Facing the burdens of this day, help me listen for the Spirit song that rises on the periphery of my attention, reminding me of your constant provision and invitation to not worry about tomorrow. Today is enough. Nurture in me the peace of silence so as to sing my own song.

Amen.

■ ■ ■

JULY 11

Turn my Martha worries into Mary peace

God Who Gives New Life:

Bless my journey as you turn my Martha worries into Mary peace. Harmonize my inner conflicts and place your hand of healing upon my interior life.

Amen.

■ ■ ■

JULY 12

Redefine my visions of success

Jesus, Servant of All:

Through faith, I ask your help to redefine my visions of success in the light of your total defeat through which the most unlikely of victories arose.

Amen.

JULY 13

You are counting out the gold of your love

Life-giving Love:

Whatever life may bring my way, you are what I am looking for.

When you are counting out the gold of your love and placing it into my hands, remind me not to look at my hands, or at the gold, but into your face.

Amen.

JULY 14

Unveil your closeness

Eternal Listener:

Unveil your closeness by Word and Spirit.

Lead me deeper into your welcome body, soul, and mind.

Amen.

JULY 15

Welcoming what is

Most Gracious and Loving Heavenly Father:

My heart rests in the peace of surrender, welcoming what is and aspiring to what may be, in and through your grace and faithful love.

Amen.

JULY 16

The way of simplicity and surrender

Beloved Spirit of God:

Teach me the way of simplicity and surrender so that in this world of consumption, noise, and endless choices I might model joy, peace, and freedom.

Amen.

JULY 17

Longings for divine union

Holy Spirit of God:

Lead me into the grace of healing.

Fill me with your peace as I feel the frictions of being human alongside the longings for divine union.

Amen.

JULY 18

Blessing versus resistance

Divine Love Speaking to My Heart:

During this summer season, give me rhythms to rest and opportunities to soak in the experience of your love through silence, nature, and reading.

Quiet the chatter of my mental conversation and concerns with the peace of your presence.

Most of all, give me the quality of relating with others that bears forth the gift of blessing versus resistance, love versus judgment.

And for my travels, I ask the grace of safety and the gift of useful surprises and new friendships, especially when stressed by the demands of unfamiliar environments, unexpected delays, difficulties, and discomforts.

In and through Christ I pray.

Amen.

JULY 19

Inspired by the encircled saints

Grace-giver:

Inspired by the encircled saints, I re-dedicate my life to the movement of your love into this and every moment of my lifetime.

Amen.

* * *

JULY 20

The purpose of my arising in life

Beloved Mind of God, in Whom I Live and Move and Have My Being:

In union with Christ, lift me up into the life of Spirit, no longer controlled by impulses to resist growth or overindulge my appetites.

Now, I choose to use all life conditions as a path to observe the way I am, not just how others are or aren't.

Aware that the purpose of my arising in life is to mature in understanding, I take responsibility for my unfolding and request teachers of wisdom to show me the way to peace and truth.

Amen.

■ ■ ■

JULY 21

Your word is made personal in the silence

Life upon Life:

I come from you and return to you and in between learn how to love. You are with me, and beyond the veil of perception I am with you.

In this moment, your welcome is available in my return and your Word is made personal in the silence.

I remember, and grow quiet on the inside, aware that my true life is hidden with you.

Amen.

■ ■ ■

JULY 22

Make me beautiful on the inside

Beautiful Savior:

You know me. I matter to you. You wish to make me beautiful on the inside, a simple reflection of your self-giving love.

I consent in silence to this interior renovation. Give me courage to observe my unloving words, gestures, and desires so I may become increasingly passive to the personality in me that wants to react, attack, or respond in the ways I have been taught by those who had forgotten love.

I belong to you. The beauty of love is my destination. Begin my second education into love by your Word and Spirit leading me deeper into your way, your truth, and your life.

Amen.

JULY 23

Feel what can't be proven

God Beyond All Comprehension:

Open me now to the gift of light, waking me up inside to a life of love, to your ever-present now and this-ness underneath and beyond all things and thoughts.

I need look nowhere else than here, now, today declared and remembered: Christ in, with, and through me by the Spirit released from death and darkness, revealed in the vast gift of the present sweetly born in silence and surrender.

I won't try to understand. I give in and descend into my heart to feel what can't be proven.

Amen.

JULY 24

Wait in silence for the clarity of your counsel

God, my Counselor:

Imprint your love upon my heart.

Lead me to walk in your light.

Guide me in all I do and say so that my words may bear witness to your way.

With your Word in my heart, I delight more than in the riches of this world.

I wait in the silence for the clarity of your counsel.

Amen.

JULY 25

You who are the first light in the depths of the deep

God of Loving-kindness:

You who are the first light in the depths of the deep, shine unexpected blessings upon my life outstretched to you.

Draw me into your closeness, and send me into the world with attentiveness to the movement of your kindness that can flow from you through me.

Amen.

JULY 26

The darkness of my fears

God My Redeemer:

Reach your hand into the darkness of my fears. Forgive my unholy ways. Let not the feeling of separation keep me from your heart. Too long have I let fear control me, projecting onto others what I am unaware of within. May your perfect love cast every fear out from the chamber of my mind and memories.

Amen.

■ ■ ■

JULY 27

Fear not the shadows of the future

You Who Birth the Future:

In your promises, I am instructed to fear not the shadows of the future, but to listen for your voice through the valleys of darkness.

Show me the path to life and the way to fullness of joy.

Remind me in prayer that your Word casts no shadows for it is the light of the world, which includes me.

Amen.

JULY 28

I am chased by your joy

God Who Brings Joy:

Touch my heartstrings and make your song come to life in me.

I am chased by your joy into new territory.

You have such a way with your extravagance.

What can I say? Phrases like “Here I am, Lord” and “Let it be in me, Lord” come to mind.

You turn my darkest howls into shouts of hosanna.

You have a way of making me your miracle.

I can see it with hindsight—always you were there, here, among the silence—infinite possibilities abounding.

Amen.

JULY 29

Your grace finds the seam in my heart

Holy Spirit of God:

Your grace finds the seam in my heart and follows it to the places waiting to be opened further by your love.

Lead me today by your gentle wisdom, guiding my way in commerce and culture.

In this silent surrender, I receive everything I need to face the next challenge.

May your grace work the seams in my heart, expanding my feeling of "I" to include the reality of you.

Amen.

JULY 30

Open hands into the morning light

God of This Moment:

I lift my open hands into the morning light to catch the present moment, this wise teacher revealing me to me.

I share my tears with the earth and remember the foundation upon which I live.

Your living Word rises up to meet me like a morning bride. Silently, suddenly you are here again in my heart awakening me for more love.

Your loving Word to be all in all.

The summertime is for loving. I walk among the dewy grass and listen to the infinite moment.

I can see in this droplet just about to release and fall to the earth itself: Weeping Spirit. Crying love. Drenching light.

And it all helps me remember.

Amen.

JULY 31

I gently place my pain with God

God of Tender Love:

When broken by life and aware of my suffering, I gently place my pain with you.

May this prayer touch the merciful hearts of Jesus and his mother in just the right way that heals old wounds, nurturing present and future growth.

Amen.

AUGUST

It is as if God says to me:

My earth speaks to you in the stillness of summer mornings.

Press your ear upon the earth. Listen to my life. You are a prayer happening forever in my heart. You are my earth's keeper.

Your Brother Tree and Sister Sky wait for you to remember my family name pressed upon your own clay flesh made alive with my Spirit.

We are in this together.

Please, go deeper now into the listening, and remember.

AUGUST 1

Let peace become my companion

Beloved Comforter:

Let your love encircle and envelop me. In your mercy raise me up. Let peace become my companion. Let me be reconciled with family and friends. May I know you, O my loving companion presence.[6]

Amen.

AUGUST 2

All things are possible

Christ My Healer:

Remind me that, with you, all things are possible. Help me not limit your power in my life today with any language of despair, restriction, or defeat.

Amen.

AUGUST 3

Cease my resistance

Beloved Trinity:

Thank you for the gift of life. Thank you for the rhythms of rest and work. Today, I request the vision to observe in myself what I so dislike in others. Give me the grace of transformation so that I cease my resistance to love in the form of judgment and dislike of others.

Amen.

■ ■ ■

AUGUST 4

Move into the future

Deep Light of the Universe:

You call me to awaken to the gift of compassion.

Soften my heart to listen with care and to look with softness.

From the beginning, you have wished for me to be and imagined who I would become.

Help me learn from the past and move into the future with the lessons of love.

Amen.

■ ■ ■

AUGUST 5

Change my heart to praise

Word Before the Beginning:

My words help shape my experience in life. Therefore I wish to notice when I am complaining or critical. Change my heart to praise and gratitude.

Amen.

■ ■ ■

AUGUST 6

I reach out to redeeming grace

Light of the World:

Dark emotions arising in reaction to difficulties in life reveal that my inner landscape is full of "towns" still in need of receiving your healing warmth. Aware of my need for help, I reach out to receive your redeeming grace.

Amen.

AUGUST 7

Your love leads me

Silent Center:

In a world seeking the summit of success, you draw me into the small, quiet shadows of surrender.

There, you teach me the way of love through the humiliations of life.

In meekness you show me joy. In surrender you show me trust. In emptiness you provide for all my needs.

I thank you that your love leads me so that I don't have to lead myself to any summit other than the hill marked with a cross, revealing the true logic of self-giving in a world addicted to winning.

Amen.

AUGUST 8

Turning me more and more into love

Beloved Christ:

Awaken in me the awareness of my tone, gesture, and word choices so that I might more completely observe how I relate to others, and in observing gain understanding, and in understanding consent to your transforming life turning me more and more into love.

Amen.

AUGUST 9

God is the fullness of meaning

Sustainer of the Created:

May the light of God surround me.

May the life of God sustain me.

May the love of God enfold me.

May the power of God protect me.

May the presence of God nurture me.

May the promises of God inspire me.

I am not alone.

My life is not meaningless.

In the beginning was meaning.

God is the fullness of meaning and through your Word I partake in this meaningful life.

And all is well.

Amen.

AUGUST 10

The house of my soul awaits your indwelling

O My Life-giving God:

The house of my soul awaits your indwelling. There are rooms that need renovation. But Lord, how can this be when I dwell in you and you in me? I wait for your arrival, only to discover you are already here with me.

Amen.

■ ■ ■

AUGUST 11

Expand my capacity to bear and share love

Loving and Holy God:

Expand my capacity to bear and share love. I know that something in me must become more like a child if I am to enter your kingdom. May this process begin with the lessening of my vanity and pride.

Amen.

■ ■ ■

AUGUST 12

Increase my desire to delight in you

Beloved Trinity:

Increase my desire to delight in you. Cleanse my will so that I desire what delights you. Fill my mind with impressions that inspire wonder so that I live in correspondence with your pulsing heart of love, radiating the beauty and joy of your intentions.

Amen.

■ ■ ■

AUGUST 13

Today, in this moment, I receive a graceful transformation

O Lord:

If it happens that during the course of this day I feel myself pressed into a particular emotion or thought, I call upon you now to remind me *then* that whatever it is that I am feeling is *not* me. Convey to me now in the silent resonance of this prayer the practical certitude I will need that my life is hidden in your life in Word and sacrament.

Today, in this moment, I request for my life a graceful transformation of water into wine, and wine into life, and life into love, and love into the light of Christ.

Amen.

■ ■ ■

AUGUST 14

Holding me together in love as I grow

Abba:

Thank you for holding me together in love as I grow. Open my heart to receive your living Word deeply. Sustain me in my life efforts so I may be refreshed by your Spirit in worship and rest.

Amen.

■ ■ ■

AUGUST 15

I wish to live the mystery of Christ

Living and Loving God:

I wish to live the mystery of Christ, not just know or speak about it. I wish for your Spirit to take hold of my life and liberate me from my fears, anxieties, demands, and desires. I wish to make Christ alive in me through relationships, respect, and self-giving. Lord, I wish to live at the growing tip of transformation, so as to no longer be the person I have always been, but to become the person you have destined me to be in Christ.

Amen.

■ ■ ■

AUGUST 16

The one necessary thing

Most Loving God:

Awake now to the gift of life, I wish to do the one necessary thing—to turn to you and your influences. Amidst all the alternatives, I choose you. Your grace and love are awakening me, turning me, softening me, and like a sunflower I respond in kind to the warmth of your light, life, and love.

Amen.

AUGUST 17

Drawn into the holiness of love

Gracious and Merciful Heavenly Father:

Pour out your Spirit upon me that I might feel your presence in the opening movements of this day. As I am drawn into the holiness of love and the strength of community, unmask my fears and worries as useless. I choose the gift of your love, and in this love I am more than a conqueror through Christ, with Christ, in Christ, in the unity of the Spirit.

Amen.

AUGUST 18

Sounding through the stars

Song of My Deepest Faith:

Help me listen to the sound of silence and feel your rhythm of grace in the movements of this day and the events of this life. Your love is the song of my deepest faith and my life is your hymn of desire sounding through the stars.

Amen.

■ ■ ■

AUGUST 19

Returning to you in surrender

Beloved One:

Bless all students returning to school.

Bless all teachers returning to teach.

Bless all leaders returning to lead.

Bless all workers returning to labor.

Bless all beggars returning for more.

Bless all hearts returning to you in surrender.

Remind us all that your gift of grace takes us all the way home.

Amen.

AUGUST 20

I feel your loving presence

Most Loving and Holy Trinity:

I wish to feel the fire of your presence radiating through me, melting away shortcomings of personality that deplete my force for love and joy. Do unto me what I cannot do for myself: heal, transform, and overcome. Such gifts are enough, Lord. I feel your loving presence and surrender my ways to your way.

Amen.

AUGUST 21

The name of Jesus fills the empty spaces

Beloved:

Nourish me in your springs of silence in the inner room of my heart, where the name of Jesus fills the empty spaces with grace, and where my consent to him leads me deeper into your Triune love.

Amen.

■ ■ ■

AUGUST 22

Under the shadow of grace

Abba:

Under the shadow of grace, I pray to discover more of the unfolding largeness of your love.

Where can I go where you are not with me?

Who can I be where you will not meet me?

Show me my fears, that I may not be driven by them. Show me where my heart closes down to love, that I may learn to open to it in the presence of fear and worry.

Thank you for Jesus, my way-shower. Taught in the silence of the heart, I learn the nature of listening for your Word so to be a vessel of grace.

Amen.

AUGUST 23

The strong circle of your way

Beloved Strength of Life:

I wish to live today in the strong circle of your way, truth, and life. But, especially, I focus today on my need to experience an inward conversion. Help me see myself more clearly today—the negative and the positive. I do not want to live in the darkness of denial. I want to live in the light of insight.

Amen.

AUGUST 24

I call to mind the beauty of wilderness

Abba:

Embraced in the personal care that I feel in places of beauty, I feel more aware that nothing can separate me from your love in Christ. I call to mind the beauty of wilderness and hold that view in my heart as an icon of your living presence.

Silence. Solitude. Expansive spaces of graceful trees—such places portend the essence of the soul, where you invite me into deeper love and life.

Amen.

AUGUST 25

The question that precedes all love

Abba:

I listen for the question that precedes all love: "Who shall I be?"

Awaken me to the feeling of "I" hidden in you.

The beginning of all things is in the silence of your heart, and I can rest there always, including right now.

Amen.

■ ■ ■

AUGUST 26

Under the shield of the name of Jesus Christ

Abiding Presence:

Remind me that under the shield of the name of Jesus Christ, all is victorious. All threads of lies and darkness are pulled back to their ends and frayed open in this name's light and love. These knots and threads no longer hold me.

Today, I wish to live under the shield of your name and in the knowledge that names are like beams of light proceeding in front of me, revealing the nature of the one referred. And your name is the eternal Word, which was in the beginning, is now, and will always be. In the name of Christ I live, and move, and have my being.

Amen.

■ ■ ■

AUGUST 27

Until the Word speaks me

Deep, Living Water:

I wish to drink from your springs of life and feel the difference your truth and love makes as you fill me with yourself, transforming me into new-creation-wine. My prayer words sound like drunkenness until shaped by grace. I shall speak them until your Word speaks me.

Amen.

■ ■ ■

AUGUST 28

Created for union with God

Christ My Love, Wisdom, and Beauty:

Help me remember that my needs for survival, power, and love do not solely define me. I am *also* created for union with you. Awaken me with your Word. Increase my hunger and thirst for your presence in the silence.

Amen.

AUGUST 29

Christ who opens

Living Gate into Abundant Life:

Where in me am I blind to your truth? Where in my life am I deaf to the calling of your living Word spoken underneath and through the silence? Aware of my human limitations, help me welcome your presence. Birth the Christ life in me today marked by the clarity of wisdom, love, and truth.

Amen.

■ ■ ■

AUGUST 30

With the dawn I rise

Holy Love, Holy God:

With the dawn I rise by the gift of your light in the face of Christ, whose love claims me this moment and lifts me up from the confusion of life into the truth of who I am and where I come from. In the hours of this day, regardless of what I am doing or where I am going, I ask for increasing purity of heart and attention to your Spirit, my inner companion of high truth and eternal love.

Amen.

AUGUST 31

Opening my heart to surrender

Eternal Listener:

I rejoice that you touch my life with a strong grace, opening my heart to surrender. It is impossible to explain. Awaiting my return, again and again your presence is asking me, "Will you love me *now*?" Yes, in this moment, I say yes to you, my source.

Amen.

SEPTEMBER

It is as if God says to me:

Return to me and let me instruct you.

Learn my wisdom that leads to freedom and my freedom that leads to love.

SEPTEMBER 1

Charged with light

Spirit of God:

Awaken me into the fullness of your knowing and lead me into the depths of your truth. Activate in my mind the capacity to understand Scripture and share love-inspired insights with others.

Amen.

SEPTEMBER 2

Release me from past shames and present fears

Almighty God, My Source and Sustainer:

Guide me on the threefold journey of purification, illumination, and union with you. Tame my passions that inhibit my flourishing and keep me asleep to the mind of your Spirit. Release me from past shames and present fears.

Amen.

SEPTEMBER 3

The center of your love

Lord Jesus, Living Christ:

In the silence, speak your Word. Transform my insecurities into empathy and my needs into miracles. In every situation that seems overwhelming to me today, let silence lead me to the center of your love and the embrace of your truth.

Amen.

SEPTEMBER 4

Transforming me further into your intention

Eternal Love and Source of Life:

Take me beneath my customary perception of Scripture to personally experience the awareness of your nearness beyond the printed page and into the mystery of faith touched by your Spirit and infused with your love, transforming me further into your intention.

Amen.

SEPTEMBER 5

The fruit of your presence

Womb of Love:

Bear in me the fruit of your presence. Show me the way to life in you as I welcome your life in me.

Amen.

SEPTEMBER 6

The mirage of my falseness

Living Forgiveness, Everlasting Grace:

Humbled by my unconscious and unloving behavior, I give thanks for the way in which life can become my teacher. I ask for the courage to see clearly through the mirage of my falseness into the truth of who I am in you, Lord Jesus Christ.

Amen.

SEPTEMBER 7

Provision upon my life today

Most Gracious and Loving Heavenly Father:

Pour provision upon my life today, grounding me in the life-giving presence of your living Word and deepening my connection with the resurrected Jesus Christ.

Amen.

SEPTEMBER 8

You have created my soul and given to me a secret strength

Most Glorious and Perfect Source of Love:

You have created my soul and given to me a secret strength—the mystery of baptism. I am flesh and spirit. Because of this, I am a hybrid, adapted for two worlds—this one of forms and feelings and your world of light and love.

Amen.

SEPTEMBER 9

The everlasting hiddenness of your love

Beloved:

I retreat deeper into your silence. There, beyond all books and beliefs, I simply feel your loving presence. "How can this be?" my soul asks. And it is as if your Spirit speaks: "Because of me. It is me. It is all me." My God, my God, you have not forsaken me! All along it has been you—higher and deeper than thought, the everlasting hiddenness of your love revealed in Christ in whom my life is now found.

Amen.

SEPTEMBER 10

Your uncommon grace pulsing through the galaxies

Loving God of the Universe:

Your journey to me has set me on a journey to you. While it is tempting to think that I am all alone on this journey, in Christ I discover that brothers and sisters of silence and spirit are with me.

Help me become a vibrant participant in this spiritual community today. Help me to see in each stranger something of myself and in so doing feel our common humanity and your uncommon grace, pulsing through the galaxies even into the realm of this beating heart.

Amen.

■ ■ ■

SEPTEMBER 11

In the remembrance

Comfort of the Suffering:

In the remembrance of moments seared with shock, I pray to connect more deeply with the meaning of life. I wish for personal knowledge and direct experience with your deepest purpose and meaning.

Hidden in the heart of this human experience is silence, and in the silence I feel your love. In the silence I discover your presence, and in your presence I find purpose.

I join my prayer today in the silence, requesting help on the journey into forgiveness and surrender, assured that humankind is being transformed from one degree of glory to another and that in Christ nothing can separate us from your loving presence—neither suffering, death, nor events past or things to come.

In holy awe for all saints and souls whose journey is now complete, I bow my heart in peace.

Amen.

SEPTEMBER 12

Feed me with your living stillness

Beloved of My Heart:

You have called me to listen. Draw me into the heart of prayer. Feed me with your living stillness. Calm me with your vast love. I request this very personal experience today. I gain strength through stillness, resting in the warmth of your name. Speak to my heart by the mystery of your Spirit, Word, and sacrament, reminding me as I go about my daily activities that you are the beloved of my heart.

Amen.

SEPTEMBER 13

Resting in you, I remember

Eternal Light of Attention:

Resting in you, I remember myself, and in so doing, I remember you. In this busy world, it is easy to forget. Today, I wish to rise in remembrance, receiving knowledge and wisdom in my heart. Although there appear to be many paths for my life, I feel drawn to this path of quietness in gentleness and surrender. Solitary in silence you kiss my soul, and I feel more alive.

Amen.

SEPTEMBER 14

Born in the mystery of your love

Joyful Song Beyond My Soul:

Born in the mystery of your love, I begin this day surrendering all my confusions and questions to your explanatory power. I request personal attention for such situations that seem bewildering to my natural mind, trusting your help will arrive.

Amen.

SEPTEMBER 15

The life hidden in the cloud of surrender

Beloved Life-giver:

I am grateful for the gift of life that is occurring in me at this moment. I stand in awe that I am sustained by your power. I recognize I am not controlling this thing called "being alive." It is a constant gift flowing to me, set in motion by your grace. I wish to use this gift of life to nourish my being and the well-being of others through the accumulation of love and wisdom. The waters of wisdom are sweet. Draw me there to be nourished by the life hidden in the cloud of surrender.

Amen.

SEPTEMBER 16

Speak to my heart in the secret chamber of the Spirit

Abba:

Speak to my heart in the secret chamber of the Spirit where I feel love and know the taste of beauty and goodness. While

I am yet a being of flesh and blood, I consent to the eternal plan for human destiny to become resonant beings of love. Even though I may not know what this means, I shall listen and wait.

My day-to-day living is full of many concerns and tasks. But you have left me a trail of living Words to lead me to yourself. Such Words are felt more than known. Explanation spoils the lion's leap. And you are leaping into my heart through silence and beauty and wisdom and love.

Amen.

SEPTEMBER 17

The blessing of assured understanding

Most Loving and Almighty God:

The world and my life situation are often cluttered with confusing choices. As I face decisions and make requests for guidance today, I ask for the blessing of assured understanding that you alone can give.

Amen.

SEPTEMBER 18

The ever-deepening experience of consciously chosen love

Beloved All in All:

I wish to feel gratitude for every person with whom I interact. I call them to mind with the eyes of my heart. I remember the ways in which I felt provoked, unaccepted, or judged, and I wish to see where I provoked, rejected, and judged others. Help me release these feelings and actions into your forgiveness, which is free and available when I look up from my toil.

Where I have felt wronged, help me forgive.

Where I have felt blessed, help me give thanks.

In all things I request the ever-deepening experience of consciously chosen love over against negative reactions.

Amen.

SEPTEMBER 19

Nurtured into the presence of your true life

Silent Embrace:

Graced by the beauty of creation, I am nurtured into the presence of your true life. Thank you for moments of wonder lost in the silence of your embrace. In the temple of my heart, I resist the temptation to *just* think about it. I wish to also feel it and experience the warming gift of your life giving love in and through every moment—all gentle invitations to surrender my striving and trust your providing.

Amen.

■ ■ ■

SEPTEMBER 20

The truth of my being one in you

Ever-living God of Peace:

Aware of the transforming power of united thoughts and feelings on a global scale, I stand in awe of my participation in and as the living, breathing body of Christ. Help me experience with direct awareness the truth of my being one with others in you. Forgive me for forgetting through regression to fear and division. I am yours, and beyond all self-generated words or pictures, you are the living source of life and love.

Amen.

■ ■ ■

SEPTEMBER 21

The shadow of your light

Beloved Silence:

Thank you for listening to my confessions and failures. Under the shadow of your light, my darkness is no more.

Amen.

■ ■ ■

SEPTEMBER 22

Stretch forth to the light through these words

Lord God of All Creation:

I confess that culture cannot satisfy the longing of my heart.

I am reaching for something more today and stretch forth into your grace through these prayer words.

You are the direction my life desires.

You are the love my being requires.

You are the light to which my soul aspires, and I praise you for meeting me with grace.

Amen.

■ ■ ■

SEPTEMBER 23

The gravity of your felt presence holds me strong

Most Loving and Gracious God:

Swayed by the speed of life, my soul feels dizzy and disoriented. Your rest beckons. The silence of your presence rises in my heart and I wish to detach from the carnival rides called life, work, and other people. Drawn by a different centrifugal force, the gravity of your felt presence holds me strong in the cycles of life. Help me rest in you, even while I also move amidst busy comings, goings, and doings.

Amen.

SEPTEMBER 24

Open to love in this world of pain

Loving God:

Help me stay open to love in this world of pain. In my hurt, I often close down. Open me with the gift of forgiveness.

In my worry, I often turn inward. Lift my gaze to your future.

In my loneliness, I often feel unworthy. Remind me of my infinite value as a participant in your divine nature.

In all things, draw me to the living love of Jesus Christ available right now in the interior realms of silence and surrender.

Amen.

SEPTEMBER 25

Awake now to the presence of your love

Beloved Lord Jesus Christ:

Awake now to the presence of your love, I feel you holding my life. I wish to see your strength reaching into the depths of my suffering. You are providing a way out, a way out that comes from above. I wish to receive this gift, and be lifted up further into the light of your wisdom, and experience the attraction to your truth and love radiating from your Word.

Amen.

SEPTEMBER 26

The delight of your living presence

Joy of My Heart, Laughter of My Soul:

Help me feel the delight of your living presence in the midst of any moments of despair. By your Spirit, fill me with a lighthearted gratefulness for the gift of life, reflecting joy in my words, gestures, and countenance.

Amen.

SEPTEMBER 27

Seal now the truths I gain this day

Beloved Presence:

Seal now the truths gained in the silence this day by the power of your Spirit so that I may rise into the one you are calling me to become. You are my God and I belong to you. Make me fully alive in you.

Amen.

SEPTEMBER 28

Drawing me closer to the center of your loving heart

Beloved Center:

I am grateful for the opportunity to remember and receive your grace. I wish to rest in you, my center, as I move about the circumference of my daily duties. In the gentle silence of prayerful moments, reveal more completely the meaning of my life, drawing me closer to the center of your loving heart, healing the self that is scattered by this life's situations, suffering, and sadness.

Amen.

SEPTEMBER 29

Let the incarnation continue

Beloved Lord Jesus Christ:

You are the living truth that brings hope here.

You are the love that brings life to bear in my barrenness.

You are the open ground from which the way is revealed.

Today, I wish to experience your truth, life, and way in direct astonishment of things revealed. In labor with angels bearing me up, I pray: let this transformation come quickly.

To the praise of your inner work in me, let the incarnation continue through me today.

Amen.

SEPTEMBER 30

Say yes to wise choices

Holy Trinity:

For you, O God, I wish to live, surrendered to your living Word helping me to say yes to wise choices with integrity, harmony, and joy.

Amen.

OCTOBER

It is as if God says to me:

Earnestly receive the colored light of this new day as my strength.

There is something to be gained in you through the silence of this pearled morning.

Listen. Wait. It is deeper than your thoughts. Feel into it through your body.

Fearlessly open to my love!

Be encouraged, not afraid, by the powers that be and always remember:

Nurture your relationship with me, your Source. All is well. Every relationship is my temple. I celebrate quality, not kind. Love is the quality of my heart, wooing you into a bigger life than you can imagine or control. Enjoy this journey, beloved ones!

Laugh from your belly. It may help loosen love and get it flowing, especially with your adversaries.

OCTOBER 1

Hold me close to your heart of love

Most Loving and Gracious God:

In my moments and hours of confusion, bring your clarity.

In my episodes of pain, bring your comfort.

In my awareness of being out of sorts, bring your peace.

I am unfolding. As I do, hold me close to your heart of love, giving me the assurance of things unseen. When day and night bring difficulties, sustain me.

Amen.

OCTOBER 2

An elegant movement in the dance of becoming

Yes, Abba, I wish to move in the circle of your truth, under the influence of your love and with the sway of your grace.

Make me an elegant movement in the dance of becoming that is the gift of your life in Christ.

Your faithfulness is cast wide in the firmament above and beneath all things. I feel its strength speaking. In this face of grace that is Christ, there is nothing that separates me from your love.

In this open circumference, help me live and move and have my being—beyond everything else I am asked, compelled, and tempted to do or be today.

Amen.

OCTOBER 3

To feel the beauty of October

Beloved Creator of the Heavens and the Earth:

I wish to feel and experience a deeper union with you. I set aside the hours of this day to feel the beauty of October and know that this season visibly demonstrates my return journey back to you.

May I be born, flourish, and release into your breath.

Amen.

OCTOBER 4

Clues to the meaning of life

Loving God:

Aware of your faithfulness to humankind, I surrender to your living Word and wisdom that are coming to me at just the right time. I thank you for these clues to the meaning of life and my purpose. Stronger together than apart, I wish to delight in you this day and know in this community of prayer that nothing can separate me from your love in Christ.

Amen.

OCTOBER 5

Open the center

Holy Spirit:

Draw me deeper into the wonder of your rest.

Whatever occurs in my external life today, I wish to remember that my inner life is hidden in God through Christ always. So it is and so it shall be.

Amen.

OCTOBER 6

I am rising this morning to receive

Eternal Love:

Your truth lights the day and your way unfolds into love.

Whatever dreams and difficulties the dark hours delivered, I am rising this morning to receive your eternal love.

Words can't capture its velocity.

Images can't contain its mass.

Your love is infinite, immediately present under, beyond, in, and through every sense, thought, and feeling I have about myself or another.

Like the sunrise, you change everything. I lift my heart in praise.

Amen.

OCTOBER 7

Anoint me with awareness

Holy Spirit of God:

Pour down upon me the rain of your life, light and love.

Anoint me with awareness.

I wait for your movements drawing me deeper into the silence of your love, making all things new.

Amen.

* * *

OCTOBER 8

The wind-word brings stillness

Holy God of My Deepening Journey:

My prayer words are meant to be like wind in tall prairie grass. The Spirit blows where it will. In my heart, there are many grasses, wheat, tares, weeds—all mixed together. Gentle are you who tends my heart, knowing one from the other. But in the open expanse of being, your words come like wind and stir the grasses, moving like waves: some smooth and stretched out, others crashing and erratic.

There is a way to stand still in the center of the vastness. Though the grass is over my head, I can feel your living words moving in my heart. The wind-words bring stillness. Feeling is beyond listening. And your Spirit is beyond the feeling. Sheer prairie presence.

Amen.

■ ■ ■

OCTOBER 9

The sum of divine oneness

Most Merciful and Loving God:

I accept the fact that I can't fix myself. So I welcome again the gift of contemplative prayer, wherein I participate in the interior experience of moving beyond faith into the sphere of your Spirit's work, multiplying even the smallest ounce of faith into the sum of divine oneness.

Amen.

■ ■ ■

OCTOBER 10

Your presence is an expanding center

Holy Love, Unending Life, Invincible Light:

I wish to enter into your house of being and sit at your banquet of wisdom. Your invitation is calling and time is a factor. While I spend much of my life and energy doing, I wish to be with you. Draw me deeper into the inner room of my heart and close the door. Your presence is an expanding center, day by day dissolving more of myself and revealing more of Christ. May I decrease, and may you increase.

In your house of being there is only one law: the law of love. Forsaken by life, I turn to your love and there find abundant life in union with Christ, who has pledged never to leave or forsake me. I need to go no farther than my breath and beating heart. I hear you now; it's as if you are saying to my soul: *Sit. Be still and understand that I am with you as holy love, unending life, invincible light.*

Amen.

OCTOBER 11

Strength to resist all temptations

Beloved Jesus, Lord of Light:

I wish to feel your life-giving presence through the gifts of silence, sermon, sacrament, and Scripture. May the beauty revealed in the undoing of summer by the forces of fall instruct me on my own spiritual journey. May this day establish me deeper in the vibrant soil of your resurrection power, offering to me strength to resist all temptations to despair of any approaching darkness.

Amen.

OCTOBER 12

Hope to hear your words of promise

Loving God:

For any difficulties I may face today, I request wisdom to see the situation from a new perspective.

For any fear I may feel today, I request peace to touch the provocation with neutralizing faith.

For any depression I may taste today, I request hope to hear your words of promise in the deep places of my being.

Draw me into silence through prayer and undo all in me that has been done to me outside the bounds of your perfect love.

Amen.

OCTOBER 13

Bring about the best possible future

Lord God of All Creation:

Anoint me with your Holy Spirit and let the mind of Christ become available to me. Open me to the unlimited possibilities of good you have in store for me. Feed me with your Spirit of wisdom, love, and understanding for each situation and person I encounter, and bring about the best possible future for my transformation in Christ.

Amen.

OCTOBER 14

On my way to the heart of God

Lord of the Seasons:

I await the revealing of barren branches and windy November nights. I feel life changing around me. I feel it in my body. Like the earth, I too am in transition: a pilgrim on my way to your heart.

I encounter sickness and am humbled; yet healing is provided.

I walk through depression and feel overwhelmed; yet new thinking emerges.

Beyond this earth there is still more of you and your creation.

Beyond all my troubles and disappointments, you are, and all is well.

Lifted up into the silent mystery of my heart unveiled to your unyielding love, I journey onward in prayer through all the seasons of this life's earthly passage.

Amen.

OCTOBER 15

Uphold me in every endeavor

Abba:

Pour out your Spirit upon my seeking mind and illuminate my path with your wisdom. Seal into my cells the radiance of your love and uphold me in every endeavor, so that I might become the fullest expression of your abundant intention for human life. Your name is "I Am," so that I might be.

I celebrate the gift of life given each moment in and through the living presence of Christ your Son, who will never leave me or forsake me. Whatever day it is, your Word says it is the same yesterday, today, and tomorrow. In you I live and move and have my being.

Amen.

OCTOBER 16

The pull of your grace

Divine Love Who Draws Me Close:

Silently draw me close by the pull of your grace, lifting me out of the gravity field of myself.

Amen.

OCTOBER 17

Bring a new and different kind of life

Light of the World:

Whatever darkness I may find in my life today, I pray to be awakened by your rays of love. Give me eyes to see the particles of praise shimmering in the sunlight of consciously chosen love. I wish to stay open-hearted even when I see the darkness, trusting that your light will illuminate my inner realms to bring a new and different kind of life.

Amen.

OCTOBER 18

Joy despite the sorrow

Lord Jesus Christ:

Let me feel your living presence as strength beneath the silence, love beyond the fear, and joy despite the sorrow.

Feed me this day with your wisdom. Cultivate in me the seed of your love that leads to deeper community. Remove in me any obstacles to love and truth.

Amen.

OCTOBER 19

Awaken to my possible evolution in Christ

God of Heaven and Earth:

The wordless wonder of your creation invites me to look up. When my own heart closes to love, remind me of the heavenly streams of creation above. Help me awaken to my possible evolution in Christ, walking with your Word and your wisdom and all those who have gone before me.

Amen.

OCTOBER 20

Clothe me in the raiment of your wisdom

God of This and Every Moment:

Clothe me in the raiment of your wisdom and bring me under the power of the cross.

In Christ, I rejoice in my freedom from whatever situation may be occurring in life.

In perfect trust, I simply give thanks for this day with joy.

Amen.

OCTOBER 21

The certitude of presence available

Lord Jesus, Living Christ:

Thank you for the certitude of presence available in the Eucharist. Thank you for the communion of saints who journey with me. Thank you for the gift of being an embodied spiritual being capable of giving, receiving, and becoming love.

Amen.

OCTOBER 22

Grounded, I can ascend

Jesus Christ, My Life:

You are teaching me that you are silent, living, and radiant. You are revealing to me that you are life from life and God from God. You are the eternal Word and the nameless name above all other names. You are helping me recognize that in you I live and move and have my being, and that this truth is the beginning of my most enduring freedom. Grounded, I can ascend.

Amen.

OCTOBER 23

My source of loving community

Loving Trinity:

Help me to meet the people and events of this day with an open heart. I wish to become love. No matter how I may be received, I thank you for being my source of loving community.

Amen.

OCTOBER 24

A temple of love

Abba:

Resting in your silence, I begin to see and feel that my heart is a sanctuary of your everlasting Spirit—a shelter for the most high, a temple of love.

I begin to participate in the sphere of wisdom, opening me to further depths of your truth.

I am a humble body, yet imbued with the music of your grace.

It is your Son who is my hymn sung through this particular chord of embodiment. The tune resonates in the central chambers, a timpanic cadence leading me back home to you with every beat.

Amen.

OCTOBER 25

A vessel of your reflected glory

Living Christ:

I pray to rise with the sun and feel your radiance in my heart. Downcast no longer, I rise with joy, love, and peace. You are giving to me the gift of consciousness, and I wish to live as a vessel of your reflected glory. Light from light, I worship you, the light of the world.

Amen.

OCTOBER 26

Transform my apparatus of perception

Abba:

Saturate my heart with the qualities of your Spirit. Draw me deeper into your presence beyond the silence. I ask for help today for all the questions I ponder and live with. Where I object to the way things are, help me to live in trust. Help me to hold my interpretations of reality loosely, gently, and humbly, in the recognition that you can transform my apparatus of perception to experience all things differently in the light of your love.

Amen.

OCTOBER 27

An unfailing guide

Beloved of My Deepest Self:

Help me to remember today that you are an unfailing guide, showing me the way through all of life's events into the peace that passes all understanding.

Amen.

OCTOBER 28

The closeness that I am

Heart of God:

Help me to see that each moment of life is an eternal gift packed with infinite possibility. Resting in the truth of self in Christ, I feel the closeness that I am in union with you by the power of the Holy Spirit. I recognize and declare that in Christ nothing can separate me from your love, and therefore I am indeed not far from your kingdom.

Amen.

OCTOBER 29

Mold the darkness of my mind

God of Now and Then, Here and There:

I wait in silence for truth to shape itself in me. Mold the darkness of my mind with the light of your wisdom, fired in the kiln of your love.

You are forming Christ in me through this journey into love, goodness, and wisdom.

Thank you for this purpose that gives holy meaning to my lifetime.

Amen.

■ ■ ■

OCTOBER 30

Living Christ, you are

Lord Jesus, Living Christ:

You are the doctor who gathers up the wounded.

You are husband, father, and brother. You are the Good Shepherd.

You are the friend of women and children and the refuge of fools and sinners.

You are the servant of servants. You are the first and last.

You are the master to whom all things are possible and in whom there is no longer anything to fear.

You are a little child, yet also the eternal Word in whom all things dwell.

You are Mary's mystery and Joseph's dream. You are my all in all.

You are the balm of broken hearts and the master of the house.

You are the speaker and the listener.

You are midwife to all souls and tender mother to all broken hearts.

You are one with the Father and you are King David's heir.

You are the light, the truth, and the way.

Your love is beyond measurement and your being is divine.

You are the suffering one who understands our human loneliness, brokenness, and betrayals.

You are the weeping one who agonizes in prayer, alone. You are one and you are the many.

You are the resurrection and the life.

You are bread and wine. You are sacrament and you are divine.

You are water-walker and wind-calmer. You are soul-doctor and Spirit-breather.

You release captives and command demons.

You are lord of the angels and ruler of the cosmos.

You are flesh and blood, but also Spirit and truth. You are faith, hope, and love. You are tears, sweat, and blood.

You are time and no-time. You are space and beyond space.

You are infinity and particle. You are consciousness and beyond. You are matter and energy.

You are no longer on the cross. You are ascended to higher realms.

You are priest for the nations and prophet for human transformation.

You are. You have been. You shall be.

You are this and so much more, and in you I shall live.

Amen.

OCTOBER 31

Connect my life with your love

God of Immense Love:

Connect my life with your love more completely, so that in the upheavals of life I feel sustained by the strength of silence.

Reveal to me the capacity of how I can further participate in what your love is doing in this incomprehensible world that meets me with joy and suffering, peace and conflict.

Through my life journeys, awaken me to become love.

Amen.

NOVEMBER

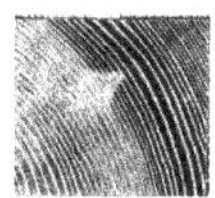

It is as if God is saying to me:

Trust me.

I'm with you through your family gatherings and holiday travels.

This is a quiet time for the earth.

Let the cold draw you deeper into the warmth of my love.

I'm right here.

NOVEMBER 1

Briefly is this way of being

Lord God of All Creation:

Every day I circle the sun on this sacred, living sphere. You have choreographed these moves, keeping good rhythm. During these longer nights and shorter days of November, kindle in my heart the light of Christ. Let this light be manifest in the form of love, wisdom, and directed living toward your blazing glory.

Thank you for the awareness of the cycles of time and the recognition that time is a factor. Briefly is this way of being; your eternity is calling. Therefore I light my candles early, rise from my cave of sleep, and surrender more and more to the light of your love in Christ.

Amen.

NOVEMBER 2

Turn my words into song sonnets

Beloved Spirit of God:

Anoint me with the silence of your strength. However this day may unfold, stabilize my heart with the ballast of Scripture.

Turn my reading into listening.

Turn my words into song.

Turn my being into becoming, lest I cease to grow.

Amen.

NOVEMBER 3

The grace of giving

Loving God:

Where I feel tangled up in wanting and constricted in love, gently open me to the grace of giving and the freedom of fellowship. When I take others negatively, help me release this way of being and receive your grace.

Amen.

NOVEMBER 4

Your life is living me

Beloved God:

Remind me that your life is living me. Your love is holding me.

Your presence is surrounding me. Your being is blessing me.

Your wisdom is guiding me. Your light is leading me.

Your creation is nurturing me. Your power is protecting me.

Your will is shaping me. Your name is claiming me.

Your Son is healing me. Your Spirit is transforming me.

How could I ever feel alone?

Amen.

NOVEMBER 5

Infuse my life with wisdom

Christ of the Ages:

Teach me to live in your joy, fearless of all that could be and courageous in all that is. May the vertical power of your cross infuse my life with wisdom beyond the powers of this external world.

Amen.

NOVEMBER 6

Rise in faith

Heavenly Father, Sustainer of This and Every Moment:

Touch my mind with the reverence that is the beginning of all spiritual wisdom and the yeast that makes me rise in faith.

Amen.

NOVEMBER 7

On this personal journey into your love

Lord Jesus Christ:

You truly contain within yourself the love I long for. Your compassion meets me in unexpected silent moments and sustains me in every dimension of my day. Where I find unfairness, bring me inner balance. On this personal journey into your love, I am set free from the demands of others' expectations and invited into the joy of simply being with you.

Amen.

■ ■ ■

NOVEMBER 8

Chance is random, but grace is certain

God of Certitude:

I wish to live under the power of your will and hold in prayer those beloved to me, near and far. Knowing that chance is random, but your grace is certain, I place myself and those I love into the certitude of your loving care.

Amen.

NOVEMBER 9

A lamp of spiritual light

God of Light:

I wish to acquire within my mind a lamp of spiritual wisdom so I will not stumble in the darkness I may confront today. Guide my steps by your Son and infuse me with the illumination Christ conveys in the Gospels, the Eucharist, and the cosmos.

Amen.

■ ■ ■

NOVEMBER 10

I am supported

God of Truth:

I wish for a mindfulness and openheartedness to your Word heard in Scripture. I request wisdom to grow in compassion toward others. In this sustaining relationship, one for the other, help me to see how I am supported by unknown brothers and sisters, especially—

Those who grow the food and supply clean water.

Those who defend and decide.

Those who drive long distances to bring milk from the farm and grapes from faraway vineyards.

Awake to the deep interconnectivity of our human system, I am humbled to play my role in the name of your love.

Amen.

NOVEMBER 11

In the circle of my friends and family

God of Life:

I pray to feel wholeness today in the circle of my friends and family. Where there are tensions, bring your peace. Where there is sickness, bring your healing. Where there is confusion, bring your clarity. Standing in your love, bring me your joy.

Amen.

NOVEMBER 12

Your sustaining web of life

God of Peace:

I wish to stand fearless in the web of your presence, assured in every season and situation that you walk with me. In every realm of reality, I am upheld by your sustaining web of life, which nurtures me into the fullness of who I am destined to be.

Amen.

NOVEMBER 13

Particular problems rise and fall

God of Insight:

I request wisdom to live in this world of relationships. Help me as problems rise and fall in my day. Help me, Lord Jesus, to love my neighbor as I love myself and to experience your peace in separating from all the thoughts and feelings that are occurring. You are with me always.

Amen.

NOVEMBER 14

A force for love

God of the Silence:

Calm and quiet my soul at the fount of your loving presence. In your silence, replenish me with a force for love, especially for those who are the most demanding. When there is nowhere else to go, inspire me to drop into my heart and find your life-giving grace there, weaving the fabric of human reality into a tapestry of love.

Amen.

NOVEMBER 15

Hear the call of your love

God of Space and Time:

Give me a listening heart to hear the call of your love. Infinite and vast, beyond all time and space, yet also right here and now, you show me there is plenty of awe to go around. Thank you for this day and all the experiences it will offer.

Amen.

NOVEMBER 16

Our extraordinary ordinariness

Almighty and Loving God:

I thank you for the gift of life. For the sake of the human community, I request that we might become the fullness of what you intend for us to be, right where we are in all our extraordinary ordinariness.

Amen.

NOVEMBER 17

Awake now to the reality

Abba:

I am awake to the reality of your emerging and eternal life happening right now in the depth of my being. I feel connected to all people and to you, in whom I live and move and have my being. My present and eternal existence is assured through this union. And so I give thanks to both know and feel these beautiful truths.

Amen.

NOVEMBER 18

More alive today than ever

Divine Teacher:

Grateful for the gift of life, I wish to feel more alive today than ever before.

Grateful for the experience of love, I wish to share more compassion.

I am aware that these gifts are to recognize, receive, and share.

Where I think these gifts have not been given, I request courage to act as if they have, and in so acting become what I think I lack.

Amen.

NOVEMBER 19

Let me become the way toward transformation

Living Christ:

I am drawn to you as your Word and grace opens my heart. I request to be fed by your love and truth. I ask to feast with you in the silence. In these approaching days of gathering with family and friends, help me exhibit an inner peace and joy.

Where there is stress, let me be the peace.

Where there is anger, let me be the forgiveness.

Where there are patterns of pain, let me become the way toward transformation.

Drawn to you at the center of my being, I surrender to the graceful possibilities you enable. For this I truly give thanks.

Amen.

NOVEMBER 20

Gather into the silence

God of Color, Warmth, and Light:

The northern nights are nearing, turning forest and field into scenes of passion.

The colored palettes of oaks and maples have sung their autumnal lullaby to summer, in tune with earthen hues of prairie grass.

It is time to gather into silence for a future season of growth.

I remember these ancient rhythms of sun and earth tilting in tandem.

I turn my heart toward your eternal home and warmth, ready for the dark night infused with your light.

Amen.

NOVEMBER 21

The solace of your company

Holy Spirit of God:

Turning now toward the solace of your company, I feel your presence and give thanks.

Be to my heart its deepest desire.

Be to my mind its fullest expression.

Be to my will its truest aim.

Amen.

■ ■ ■

NOVEMBER 22

Embraced in the center of your encompassing truth

Living One Whose Love Pulses Through the Creation:

Embraced in the center of your encompassing truth, I discover that in you there is no circumference. You can take it all. You embrace all dimensions of myself and awaken me further into your way, your truth, and your life. In Christ, show me how your love pours into this sphere of life, intersecting as a cross, embracing my humanity—all of it.

Amen.

NOVEMBER 23

Your eternal love leaps long into the history of things

I offer no resistance to you, O Lord my God, for from your creative power flash forth the particles of light that form into stars and galaxies.

From your Word comes forth the foundation for all life and beauty, inspiring curiosity and adoration among the attentive.

I offer no resistance to you, O Lord my God, for your eternal love leaps long into the history of things, a kindness for the human species formed in your image.

On this day, I surrender completely and humbly to the facts that I am yours and life is a gift.

For every delight I experience as a member of the human community, I give thanks.

For every suffering I seek to avoid but yet encounter, I give thanks. All of life is a gift. With tenderness, with joy, and with laughter.

In awe for all the ways life supports humankind, and all the ways we can support one another, I give thanks. I feel grateful in many ways, but it is mostly like this: To be a human is to feel that rising in my chest that tastes sweet and gentle all at once. To be human is to know that I can't explain our own existence.

These are some things—ancient things—that inspire me today with praise and prayer. My guard is down now, Lord. Enter in.

Amen.

NOVEMBER 24

Into days of feasting

O Lord God with and Through Us:

As I enter into days of feasting, help me create space for your presence.

As I partake in days of travel, help me take time for rest.

As I reunite with family, help me see in myself the thing I secretly or blatantly resist and by which I judge them.

Help me become love in the ordinary gathering of people, friends, neighbors, and family.

Amen.

■ ■ ■

NOVEMBER 25

The bread of everything

God of my Gratitude:

In thanksgiving and praise I find a clue to the meaning of my life; a crumb from the bread of everything. I taste and see Mother's tears shed under the star of Bethlehem and in the shadow of the cross. What mystery did she know of this secret indwelling of the most high? What might I too discover in the silence of all the ages past now lifted up to my lips in the cup of Christ's presence? Fed by love, help me lift my heart in service to the hungry and forsaken too.

Amen.

NOVEMBER 26

So to remain at center

Living Life and Sustaining Love:

Help me feel your attracting grace in the universe, which keeps everything from coming apart. May the Word of Christ hold me together with wisdom and love. I give thanks for your Word and consent to being held by it so to remain at center with you.

Amen.

NOVEMBER 27

Your center expands to my circumference

Beloved Companion of My Heart:

Your center expands to my circumference and I feel alive again.

Your life keeps me connected beyond my immediate concerns in order to love and serve you and others.

From the gift of your recharging love I am filled to share, and for this I truly give thanks.

Amen.

NOVEMBER 28

My full attention

Most Gracious God of Love:

You have journeyed with me through this year of Sundays—Epiphany, Easter, Ascension, Pentecost, and the long stretch of ordinary green growth. Now I approach the candles of Advent.

I wish to give you my full attention so I may experience your fullness of life. As I enter through the gates of thanksgiving into the kingdom of Advent, reign in love on the throne of my heart, anointing me with the name Emmanuel.

Amen.

NOVEMBER 29

The overshadowing presence of Spirit

Holy God, Name Beyond All Names:

Your love announces to my innermost fears and insecurities an intention to transform me into a vessel of your life.

With Mary I surrender to the overshadowing presence of Spirit raising me to meet any unexpected events as a bearer of Christ.

Through this silent formation you touch my life so deeply that a new name appears upon the mantel of my heart, manifesting security and fearlessness beyond my capacity to create.

I praise you for naming me as a child of the most high.

Amen.

NOVEMBER 30

To live amidst the shadows of the past

Light of the World:

Open my heart and open my mind to your goodness and love.

Show me the way to live amidst the shadows of the past in the light of your forgiveness.

Amen.

DECEMBER

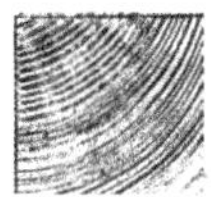

It is as if God is saying to me:

You now enter into the deepest days of darkness.

Take time to recall through story and song the message of my descent to you in love.

While it's an ancient story told with the poetry of a different era, remember this: I surprise with wonder. I make the impossible, glorious.

Watch. Wait. Wonder.

DECEMBER 1

The coming of Christ

Abba:

Unwrap the layers of my heart in these Advent days so I can more clearly see the presence of your Christ in both friend and stranger.

Amen.

DECEMBER 2

Your appearing in others

Loving God:

I make this my prayer today. I wish to know your closeness.

I will watch for your appearing in others and say with Mary, "Let it be with me according to your word."

Amen.

DECEMBER 3

I await your return to the world

Lord Jesus Christ:

I give my heart to the loving attention of your living presence within. Help me build my life upon the security of your Word in this uncertain world. I confess I need Advent to remind me that you are coming to me. Enduring and eternal, your Spirit upholds all things and dwells within. Be born again through me. In this surrendered heart, I await your return to the world.

Amen.

■ ■ ■

DECEMBER 4

A gift of mercy

Living Christ:

I wish to be a gift of mercy and compassion today. You, O Lord Christ, are here, calling me into love and holiness.

Amen.

DECEMBER 5

May this Advent season crescendo

Living God of the Liturgy:

May this Advent season crescendo with luminosity, bearing the light of Christ made beautiful by love through humbled hearts.

No longer just poetry or song, I awake to the personal pageant of your birth in me today. Infused with Advent beauty, I feel your loving presence. Your prophets are calling. You are preparing a space for grace in me. I willingly surrender.

Amen.

■ ■ ■

DECEMBER 6

The shelter of the living Christ

God of the Humble:

With Mary, the mother of Jesus, I dedicate my inner being to the shelter of the living Christ. Overshadow me with your Spirit of life and bring to bear through me this day a further incarnation of light, life, and love.

Amen.

■ ■ ■

DECEMBER 7

I ride the moment into the future

Beloved of My Lifetime:

My heart is alive with a desire reflected in the nighttime heavens. Alive, awake, shining, I ride the moment into the future with a faith grounded in that first kiss from your love, when as a child I looked up and saw a shooting star and felt the falling snowflake come to rest on my cheek.

Amen.

■ ■ ■

DECEMBER 8

We the simple and unadorned

Lord Jesus, Living Christ:

Let it be in us according to your Word.

We the simple and unadorned.

We the masses.

We the worker bees.

We the day laborers for life.

We the weary mothers and fathers.

We with calloused hands and soft hearts.

We shall be your glorious temple, and we will practice today with prayer.

Amen.

DECEMBER 9

You presence over presents

Coming King of Love:

I wish to feel your living presence in and through me in these Advent days, so as to be alert for the celebration of your birth, then, now, and yet to be. I choose a conscious Christmas, attentive to your Word in me and not to the chatter of our culture. I choose your presence amidst presents.

Amen.

■ ■ ■

DECEMBER 10

The light, life, and love of my inner world

Light of the World:

As I wait for your appearing, I observe in the darkness secrets, sorrows, and shadows.

May secrets lurking in the underside of my soul be revealed in the presence of your light.

May sorrows heavy-laden upon my heart be relieved by the presence of your life.

May the shadows cast by gnarled memories be smoothed out in the presence of your love.

Through and in Christ, who is the light, life, and love of my inner world.

Amen.

■ ■ ■

DECEMBER 11

Light my candles of faith

Faithful God:

Whatever happens in the world, your light of wisdom and love endures. In this partnership with humankind, you provide strength, safety, and sustenance. Therefore, I will not fear. I celebrate and light my candles of faith.

Amen.

■ ■ ■

DECEMBER 12

Inspired by your initiative

Divine Love:

Pour into the vessel of my heart the presence of love for you and others. Inspired by your grace, I choose to become a living gift of love today. Freed from all compulsion to demand proof of another's worthiness, I simply offer the free gift of love, in word, deed, and countenance.

Amen.

DECEMBER 13

Further into the deepening darkness

Lord Jesus, Living Christ:

Each day I draw further into the deepening darkness. I await your light of the world. The darkness has its limits. The earth will tilt again and the light will rise.

I give to you, Lord Jesus Christ, my self-contained fears and desires; while my interior remains hidden to others, it remains open to the light of your love.

Amen.

DECEMBER 14

Become the joy no red wine can give

God of Miraculous Events:

In the darkness of these days, I enter the center of the flame of your Christ's love. In this light, I open to your love and taste the joy no red wine can give. More alive than ever, I pray to not spend my days curled up on the inside with wanting. Help me live with an open heart bearing love in ordinary ways.

Amen.

DECEMBER 15

Jesus's birth is a demonstration

God of Wondrous Ways:

In the confusion of commerce and over years of myth-making, it is easy for my mind to wander from the intention of Christmas. Open my heart and mind to the truth hiding in plain sight: Jesus's birth is a demonstration of what you wish to do through each of us.

In him, your love embraced humanity.

In him, nothing can now separate us from your love.

I surrender to your continuing incarnation through me.

Amen.

DECEMBER 16

Your love is vast, infinite, and available

Lord God of All Creation:

The longest night nears, but so too does your light in Christ.

For all my moments of stress spent shopping or in crowds, I receive your peace.

For all those who wonder how to make ends meet, I request your provision.

For all those who feel lonely, I request your loving presence.

All is well, beyond every perception to the contrary. Help me see how your love is vast, infinite, and available in the tender darkness of surrender, prayer, and praise.

Amen.

DECEMBER 17

The glorious impossible

God of Possibilities:

A week from today I will rest this busy body and watch children, friends, and family open presents. It will be Christmas Day. All my preparations will be complete.

I give you every concern that overwhelms and every relationship that is rusty. I invite your possibilities to continue in my life and loved ones. In your grace, do the glorious impossible.

Amen.

■ ■ ■

DECEMBER 18

An interior Christmas

Lord Jesus, Living Christ:

You are the universal letter, addressed to everyone. It is felt and opened up to. I request the personal experience of your continuing presence. Lead me from confusion to clarity through the silence. You are as near as the love I feel in my chest. You are as close as the laughter in my belly. You are with me as the light for thought and breath for life. Today I choose an interior Christmas, connected in my body to Bethlehem and with heaven in my heart.

Amen.

DECEMBER 19

Shadows cast by traumas past

Light of the World:

May your Word reveal to me the path to wisdom and love in all my relationships and choices.

Where there is darkness in my personality and shadows cast by traumas past or anxieties present, ever so gently illumine these opportunities in the light of your silent grace.

May your love made personal through Christ by the Spirit in Word and sacrament, lead me to participate more deeply and sincerely in the journey into your union with me.

Amen.

DECEMBER 20

The mystery of Christmas

Beloved of Bethlehem:

A few days from today, Lord, I will grow silent in awe of the mystery of Bethlehem. Help me prepare to receive your living Word again.

Amen.

DECEMBER 21

I enter into the deepest days of darkness

Light of the World, Glory of the Heavens:

I enter into the deepest days of darkness in this season of lights and love.

I anticipate the coming of your Christ declared by prophets and recalled through story—and also occurring right now in my receptive heart of faith.

Help me connect more deeply with your love for humankind in Christ.

Give me courage to be the love that Jesus bore witness to and invites all of us to become.

Amen.

■ ■ ■

DECEMBER 22

I offer my total being to your total grace

All Praise to You, O God of Love:

I offer my total being to your total grace.

With Mary, I wish to sing a song of love's freedom, of light's wisdom, of life's unfolding.

By your overshadowing Spirit of creation let my will, imagination, and memory become virgin again.

Let water, sky, and earth become virgin again.

Let a second innocence return, now christened with the consciousness of two thousand years of life experience in the age of Eucharist and Spirit.

I see that our ways of division, war, greed, and fear were never our destiny and will not limit our becoming.

Let this Advent prepare me and the world in the most practical ways to go deeper into the self being born by your Word to a united destiny in love.

Amen.

DECEMBER 23

Deeper into your story of love

Abba:

I lift my dreams to you. Help me listen for your leading in the stillness of my sleep. Prepare my life to receive your Word again. Help me see deeper into your story of love and participate with faith.

Amen.

DECEMBER 24

The ecstasy of love leaps forth through eternity into time

The sound of silence opens into song, with stars leading to the light of the world made visible in the human field of flesh and form. This ecstasy of love leaps forth through eternity into time, to be for us the hope of love lived to give all for all that it may become the all in all.

The Spirit births again for each of us an upright bearing toward this light, life, and love through our threefold family name: Father, Son, and Holy Spirit. Opening us, the gift rises through the centuries, undoing the self that strikes out in fear, judgment, and wanting. Freed to love, we now can sing the personal song of the hierarchies made flesh in us: *Hosanna to God in the highest. Glory and power and might are yours, now and forever. Your love triumphs through humility. Our soul knows its worth and falls on its knees. Silent night, holy night, your new song sings me!*

Amen!

DECEMBER 25

Christmas is for everyone

God of Bethlehem:

Christmas is for the depleted, defeated, and destroyed.

It is for the burdened, barren, and beaten down.

Christmas is for the poor, outcast, and prisoner.

Christmas is for the hungry, oppressed, and refugee.

Christmas is for the empty, poured out, and broke.

Christmas is for the evicted and the laid-off. It is for the bankrupted, jobless, and homeless.

Christmas is for the ill, bedridden, and locked up.

Christmas is for the abandoned, hopeless, and depressed.

Christmas is for the sick, weak, and dying.

Christmas is for the elderly, the alone, and the weary.

Christmas is for the orphans and the unborn.

Christmas is for travelers, the stranded, and the waiting.

Christmas is for the convicted, the caught, and the anxious.

Christmas is for the guilty, the frauds, and the unjust. It is for the divorced and the miserable. It is for the occupied, the invaded, and the terrorized.

Christmas is for the Third World and the forgotten. It is for the thirsty, hungry, tattered, and unclothed.

And also:

Christmas is for the uplifted, victorious, and enduring. It is for the lighthearted, fruitful, and lifted up.

Christmas is for the wealthy, the famous, and the free.

Christmas is for the fed, the powerful, and the oppressor.

Christmas is for the full, the overflowing, and the put-together.

Christmas is for the homeowner and the employed. It is for the billionaire and the boss. It is for the healthy, vibrant, and free.

Christmas is for the friended, the hopeful, and the joyful.

Christmas is for the healthy, the strong, and the living.

Christmas is for youth, for families, and for the energized.

Christmas is for the adopted and the born.

Christmas is for the homebound, the befriended, and those who have arrived.

Christmas is for the innocent, the free, and the peaceful.

Christmas is for those with clear consciences, the authentic, and the just. It is for the married and the joyful. It is for the occupiers, the invaders, and the terrorizers.

Christmas is for the First World. It is for all who are remembered. It is for the quenched, satisfied, stable, and clothed.

Christmas is for everyone.

Every human being, every living thing. Every place. Every Person. Every time.

Christmas is here, there, and everywhere. Everything past, present, and future.

Christ is all in all. Christ is your Yes to us. You are, thus we shall be.

Christmas is for love.

Christmas is love.

Christmas is.

Christmas.

Christ.

Love.

I welcome your divine love and blessings to, for, and in all these ways of being human.

Amen!

DECEMBER 26

Encircled by eternity

Sphere of Being, Dancing Love:

Encircled by eternity, lift me up into your love. Flowing through existence is your living and active Word, sustaining and upholding all things, including me. I am part of your fabric of divine intention, a participant of your holy web of emerging life. I consent to the victory of love in Christ, then, now, and always.

Amen.

DECEMBER 27

I turn my heart to the warmth of your love

Source of Song and Light of Love:

I lift my silence in praise to thee.

You hold the mysteries of the heavens and manifest the gift of light through all suns and stars above and sons and daughters below. May your kingdom come on earth as it is in the heavens. On this winter day, I turn my heart to the warmth of your love to melt away the barriers to your way and will. In my simple and silent surrender, help me become what I already am—your light-bearing heir.

Amen.

DECEMBER 28

The faithfulness of God is occurring

Unending Strength of Love:

When I am faced with mounting debts, sickness, or personal difficulties it is easy to forget that you, my God, are working. Help me to see that your faithfulness is occurring, despite my inability or unwillingness to perceive under the surface the mystery of your glory rising through this momentary suffering or lack.

Amen.

■ ■ ■

DECEMBER 29

The undivided wholeness in which I live

Loving God with Us:

Open my heart and mind to feel your presence and my existence in you. Help me release fears, wants, and judgments that separate others into parts and perceptions limiting my experience of oneness with you and others.

Draw me into the hidden life of Christ who is all in all, connecting through wholeness the many into one body of love, bringing to all the personal quality of presence in and acceptance of that which is occurring right now.

Amen.

■ ■ ■

DECEMBER 30

The speed of seasons

Voice of Silence:

I wait for your hand to move at the speed of seasons coming to their full in the perfect synchronicity of divine providence, tuned to the time of unfolding grace meeting me face to face in Scripture and silence.

Amen.

* * *

DECEMBER 31

An imprint of wholeness in community

Lord God Almighty:

It's as if you are saying to me, *Plumb the silence and find me. Explore my grace and discover yourself again. Rest in me, and watch me do my miracles in the life from me that is now your own.*

And my heart cries out: O my Beloved! Unveil the secret of your hidden love at the center of my being. Turn this new year into a time and space for oneness—with you, with others, and with the real "I" in me who wishes to be born solid through the multiplicity of my persona.

Beyond just me, birth the real "us" that can be for the world an imprint of wholeness in community held by the bond of your love, vivified by the warmth of your good, true, and Holy Spirit.

Amen.

PRAYERS FOR HOLY DAYS AND SEASONS

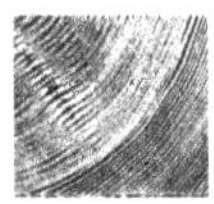

Through the Seasons in Love and Silence

Day encircles light,
Night the scarce space.

Linger with me at center;
feel my life become yours,
and then mine again.

I whisper your name
underneath the rock's silence;
everlasting is my resting.

Come to me and listen.
My heart presses upon your waiting.

This is home,
Together.

And the Spirit Says:

Take my hand and feel the grip of nothing that holds everything with light and moves with grace and slight rhythms. Take my hand and release your grip on everything else, grasping at nothing but surrender.

And in your empty palms pressed together at the heart, feel the arrival of love's warmth as fear and other such soul-fevers slip through the lattice clasp of wanting desire.

Take the hands of everyone else and place them to your face, as a blind beggar looking for someone long lost; remember who you are and what all life is for.

I am the hand of God worn smooth with loving touches caressed in prayer—empty always, yet filled with giving.

I am left and right; presence and absence; illumination and transformation. I am two hands, building a temple for your wishes. I use every tear for mortar, every laugh for stone.

These hands are ceaseless, though never weary. They move out over all things as wind, wisdom, light, song.

And hold fast to you now, always, in right or wrong.

Amen.

CHRISTMAS

Word made flesh;
Life refreshed.
Love, to us now given.

God drew near;
Joy, not fear.
Love, to us now given.

Wonder how?
Heart must bow.
Love, to us now given.

Enter King;
Miracle gifts bring.
Love, to us now given.

Wrapped in words;
Opened when heard.
Love, to us now given.

Word for me;
Stable to Tree.
Love, to us now given.

I am part of your living Word from the beginning. Perhaps this might change my plans for today—or even for tomorrow. I ponder and listen again to the ancient gift hidden within me—and wish to be opened by your love:

My body, Bethlehem.

My mind, a manger.

My heart, a hymn of praise in tempo with your Spirit.

Amen.

NEW YEAR'S EVE PRAYER

Lord Jesus Christ:

With you, I journey.

In your humanity, I am.

In your divinity, I shall be.

Released from the maze of memories written in the past, I am lifted up into a renewed freedom to love.

Drawn to you by the magnetism of grace, I conclude this year with gratitude, and begin the New Year trusting your faithfulness to bring about my deepest aims.

Amen.

ASH WEDNESDAY

God of Transformation:

You set our hearts on fire with the personal touch of your Spirit enfolding truth into our minds as an impression of wisdom.

You enliven us with your love that we know beyond knowing. Your unstoppable impulse to share your life with us is available at this moment, inviting us forward into this Lenten way.

Amen.

And now, O God of perfect timing, enter into each of our hearts and find the city-center in us ready to receive and surrender to your love in its embodied form and in its eternal formlessness.

We have been preparing for the entrance of your Word through this Lenten journey and now we feel your timeless approach nearing. What are you calling us to do? What more can we surrender of our self? How can we live with this exquisite wound of love that suffering teaches?

This city-center is the ongoing temple of our heart, mind, and soul, today arranged and set apart to celebrate your arrival.

Your way shows us that soon your arrival will require surrender, and in this surrender there will be great suffering.

Yet, so too your truth shows us that in this suffering there will be something gained on behalf of others, and through this gain of love a power untold will pierce through the field of appearances and birth a new life through all that is dead and dying in us.

And so it is that your life is felt more fully in our welcoming all things, but especially the body and blood of the Eucharist as the ongoing teacher and embrace of your joyful presence.

Amen.

MAUNDY THURSDAY

Lord God of All Creation:

Every night reminds us of the darkness that we can't escape, yet tonight the darkness is particularly deep.

Infused with betrayal, laced with denial, sealed with the cup, marked with Gethsemane blood, you, Lord Jesus Christ, embraced surrender while rejecting the way of the sword. You entered into the valley of the shadow of death, meeting betrayal, denial, rejection, conviction, abandonment in order to join human nature in the depths of its dysfunction and rejection of love.

Evil is the denial of ultimate Reality. Tonight, we prepare to see the depths of unreality: unbelief, hatred, and violence.

Lord Jesus, the drama is enacted in your life to show us what is in our life. Exposed to the light of your surrendering yet pursuing love, we hear the clank of keys coming down the dark prison hallway of the night that lets the prisoners know they can be free. It sounds like this: "*Father, forgive them for they know not what they do.*"

Amen.

GOOD FRIDAY

My God, My God of All My Why's:

It is now finished. This is the hour. The moment when selfhood became lost into your hands, and your hands became remembered in a human body. One with you in Christ, humanity can never be separated again.

I need not wonder how it is done, only request the grace to surrender to let it be done unto me: dead to self, alive to you.

Amen.

HOLY SATURDAY

Lord Jesus, Living Christ:

On your inward journey into the depths of being and beyond, reveal in each of us the places where there are still captives that need to hear your story and be set free. Descend all the way down into the thinking and doing that is resistant to your love. We need your help to be raised back to life not just tomorrow but right now, finally set free from our self-bound ways of fear and falseness. From that moment of integration with your love, we will truly live. You are indeed our hope of true glory, then, now, and always.

Amen.

EASTER SUNDAY

O God of the Light, Bearer of the Heavens:

Your life, light, and love have once and for all permeated through the veil of human flesh into the fullness of the cosmos through the personal location of resurrection in the historical human Jesus of Nazareth. We wish to participate in the ongoing flourishing of human nature in union with the resurrection of Christ, pouring out into the realm of human relationships interconnected with you by the Spirit through the Eucharist and the mystery of oneness.

In our world of death, suffering, and sorrow, you have sounded a new octave of life, reverberating through the cosmos in each dimension and direction. Give to each of us the full capacity to consent to this signal sound permeating with the harmonics of love, seen and unseen. We wish to not only hear it but be the very vessel in which the sound is turned into form.

When this truthful sound lands in each of us, stabilize us with the wisdom of Scripture and the strength of community so that we are not undone by the glory of the event. Show us the way in our study and encounter with the living Christ through our silence in prayer and exclamation in praise.

In, through, and with Christ, for the hope of the creation and all whose hearts are warmed by the felt touch of love and know beyond knowing that nothing now can separate us from the love of God in and through the risen and ongoing Christ.

Amen.

PENTECOST

Holy Spirit of God:

I rest in your continued anointing.

By your Spirit, guide my intellect to wisely see and know.

Direct my will to harmoniously choose and act.

Open my heart to relentlessly love and serve.

Since through Christ by the Spirit you are in me and I am in you, connect me also with others so that your kingdom might come again through us, your living body of light continuing on this earthly sojourn.

Amen.

THANKSGIVING

O God Who Sustains All in Every Way:

Over the circled space of this solar orb since we last gathered to give thanks, we look to the depths and see reasons both clearly and dimly to doubt the goodness of life—sickness, pain, suffering, disaster, depression, layoffs, and diagnosis. All have been in our midst.

We look to the heights and see in realms of love the truth that we are and have been sustained through all such depths by means of the gift of one another. We remember the unexpected blessings, the births, the weddings, the successes, and the quiet moments of peace, love, joy, and beauty.

We look to the width and breadth of our being human and see in the faces of those we love a mirrored reminder of who we are and who we can more fully become.

Holding hands now we feel the assurance that we are more alive together than apart. We sense the common human bond of being, this gift that rises and falls yet never ceases to teach and woo us into our God-intended destiny.

You, O Lord our God, are wishing us to be. In this silence, we feel the holiness of our time touching your eternity. We bend the heart toward gentleness, surrendering our resistance to love a little more. It's as if we hear you saying to us, "Give in. Go all the way to love itself."

Opening to you in this silence of prayer, we let go of the resentments. We release the tears that mark the forgotten stories. We reconcile with the losses, the damage, the baggage, and the prodigals. We all are welcomed home in this love made manifest together. We are a tapestry story of your total grace.

In the bond of the breath of God, in this name sealed upon our hearts in gratitude, we say "Yes!" by saying "Thank you!"

Amen.

AT A TIME OF DEATH

Nearing the door of death, please greet me with your loving light. I hope to hear your ocean song calling me home, when all that has not been done is surrendered. Help me recognize that I am free to sink away into the depths of your love, no longer just as me, but also as another wave returning home to you.

Amen.

■ ■ ■

AT A TIME OF DECISION

In the silence may your Word wake me with the light of love guiding my way home. Help me remember who I am and recognize my fears as shadows dispelled by the dawn of your wisdom drawing near to my heart.

Amen.

Notes

January 30

An event inspired this prayer: I spoke with a young husband who told me that, as he was driving to the hospital at four in the morning to see his wife, who was in cardiac arrest, he heard her voice as the car radio came on. Her voice said, "Beloved, I must go now." It was 4:42 AM. Later, when he was speaking with the doctors, they confirmed that it was at that precise time that his wife died.

May 1

Nan C. Merrill, *Psalms for Praying: An Invitation to Wholeness* (New York: Continuum, 2008). Adapted from Psalm 31.

June 17

The first four "Let me" lines of this prayer are inspired by the contemplative Bernadette Roberts, who shared this during a private retreat in Fullerton, California, November 7, 2010. She said that this is the prayer she says with her grandchildren as she tucks them into bed.

July 3

Adapted from the Carmina Gadelica prayer "Encompassing," in Esther De Waal, *The Celtic Way of Prayer* (New York: Doubleday, 1999).

August 1

Merrill, *Psalms for Praying*. Adapted prayer from Psalm 88.

Further Resources

BOOKS

Richard J. Foster and Emilie Griffin, eds. *Spiritual Classics: Selected Readings on the Twelve Spiritual Disciplines*. New York: HarperCollins, 2000.

Frederica Mathewes-Green, *The Jesus Prayer: The Ancient Desert Prayer that Tunes the Heart to God.* Brewster, Massachusetts: Paraclete Press, 2009.

Thomas Keating. *Open Mind, Open Heart: The Contemplative Dimension of the Gospel.* New York: Continuum, 1994.

Nan C. Merrill, *Psalms for Praying: An Invitation to Wholeness*. New York: Continuum, 2008.

Mark Nepo, *The Book of Awakening: Having the Life You Want by Being Present to the Life You Have.* San Francisco: Conari Press, 2000.

INTERNET

www.ContemplativeChristians.com

www.Facebook.com/groups/ContemplativeChristianity

www.ContemplativeOutreach.org

About Paraclete Press

WHO WE ARE

As the publishing arm of the Community of Jesus, Paraclete Press presents a full expression of Christian belief and practice—from Catholic to Evangelical, from Protestant to Orthodox, reflecting the ecumenical charism of the Community and its dedication to sacred music, the fine arts, and the written word. We publish books, recordings, sheet music, and video/DVDs that nourish the vibrant life of the church and its people.

WHAT WE ARE DOING

Books

PARACLETE PRESS BOOKS show the richness and depth of what it means to be Christian. While Benedictine spirituality is at the heart of who we are and all that we do, our books reflect the Christian experience across many cultures, time periods, and houses of worship.

We have many series, including *Paraclete Essentials*; *Paraclete Fiction*; *Paraclete Poetry*; *Paraclete Giants*; and for children and adults, *All God's Creatures*, books about animals and faith; and *San Damiano Books*, focusing on Franciscan spirituality. Others include *Voices from the Monastery* (men and women monastics writing about living a spiritual life today), *Active Prayer*, and new for young readers: *The Pope's Cat*. We also specialize in gift books for children on the occasions of Baptism and First Communion, as well as other important times in a child's life, and books that bring creativity and liveliness to any adult spiritual life.

The MOUNT TABOR BOOKS series focuses on the arts and literature as well as liturgical worship and spirituality; it was created in conjunction with the Mount Tabor Ecumenical Centre for Art and Spirituality in Barga, Italy.

Music

The PARACLETE RECORDINGS label represents the internationally acclaimed choir *Gloriæ Dei Cantores*, the *Gloriæ Dei Cantores Schola*, and the other instrumental artists of the *Arts Empowering Life Foundation.*

Paraclete Press is the exclusive North American distributor for the Gregorian chant recordings from St. Peter's Abbey in Solesmes, France. Paraclete also carries all of the Solesmes chant publications for Mass and the Divine Office, as well as their academic research publications.

In addition, PARACLETE PRESS SHEET MUSIC publishes the work of today's finest composers of sacred choral music, annually reviewing over 1,000 works and releasing between 40 and 60 works for both choir and organ.

Video

Our video/DVDs offer spiritual help, healing, and biblical guidance for a broad range of life issues including grief and loss, marriage, forgiveness, facing death, understanding suicide, bullying, addictions, Alzheimer's, and Christian formation.

Learn more about us at our website:
www.paracletepress.com,
or call us toll-free at 1-800-451-5006.

You may also be interested in . . .

Be Still and Listen

Experience the Presence of God in Your Life

AMOS SMITH

FOREWORD BY
PHILEENA HEUERTZ

AFTERWORD BY
DALE HANSON BOURKE

ISBN 978-1-61261-865-4 | $16.99
Trade paper

The various crises we experience in society and culture today, at their root, reveal a spiritual problem: a profound lack of meaning. The mystical truths revealed in scripture can surely help.

Part One, "Entering the Desert," introduces the reader to principles of awareness, deep listening, and contemplation as essential for "hearing" what Scripture has to say. Part Two details the importance of mystery and struggle in the process of healing from any past or present wounds. And Part Three explores the "undivided heart" that is possible when we come to know God in silence and stillness.

With *Be Still* it is possible to explore the contemplative dimensions of the Bible, either on your own or in a group setting, as you perhaps never have before.